Word of Life

LUTHER, MELANCHTHON POMERANUS AND CRUCIGER.
THE REFORMERS OF GERMANY.

This lithograph by William Henry Simmons (copying a painting by
Pierre-Antoine Labouchère) was published around 1870 and depicts (from left
to right) Philip Melanchthon, Martin Luther, Johannes Bugenhagen, and
Caspar Cruciger Sr. working on revisions of the German translation of the
Bible. See Gerhard Schwinge, Melanchthon in der Druckgraphik: Eine
Auswahl aus dem 17. Bis 19. Jahrhundert (Ubstadt-Weiher: Verlag
Regionalkultur, 2000), 108–9.

Word of Life

Introducing Lutheran Hermeneutics

TIMOTHY J. WENGERT

FORTRESS PRESS
MINNEAPOLIS

WORD OF LIFE
Introducing Lutheran Hermeneutics

Print ISBN: 978-1-5064-0282-6
eBook ISBN: 978-1-5064-0283-3

Cover image: Illustration by Amy Giacomelli
Cover design: Laurie Ingram

Contents

Abbreviations

AL   *The Annotated Luther*. Edited by Hans Hillerbrand et al. 6 vols. Minneapolis: Fortress Press, 2015–2017.

Ap   Apology of the Augsburg Confession.

BC   *The Book of Concord*. Edited by Robert Kolb and Timothy J. Wengert. Minneapolis: Fortress Press, 2000.

CA   The Augsburg Confession.

CO   *Ioannis Calvini Opera Quae Supersunt Omnia*. 59 vols. Edited by Wilhelm Baum, Eduard Cunitz, and Eduard Reuss. Braunschweig, Leipzig, and Zurich, 1834–1900.

CR   *Corpus Reformatorum: Philippi Melanthonis opera quae supersunt omnia*. Edited by Karl Bretschneider and Heinrich Bindseil. 28 vols. Halle: A. Schwetschke & Sons, 1834–1860.

LC   Large Catechism

LW   *Luther's Works* [American edition]. Edited by Jaroslav Pelikan et al. 82 vols. planned. Philadelphia: Fortress Press; St. Louis: Concordia, 1955–1986; 2009–.

MSA   *Melanchthons Werke* [Studienausgabe]. Edited by Robert Stupperich. 7 vols. Gütersloh: Bertelsmann, 1951–1975.

SA   Smalcald Articles.

SC   Small Catechism.

WA   *Luthers Werke: Kritische Gesamtausgabe [Schriften].* 65 vols.
Weimar: H. Böhlau, 1883–1993.

WA Bi   *Luthers Werke: Kritische Gesamtausgabe: Bibel.* 12 vols.
Weimar: H. Böhlau, 1906–1961.

WA Br   *Luthers Werke: Kritische Gesamtausgabe: Briefwechsel.* 18
vols. Weimar: H. Böhlau, 1930–1985.

Preface

"The history of the church [is] the history of the interpretation of Holy Scripture."[1] With this insight Gerhard Ebeling explained his groundbreaking work in a new field of study in church history: tracing the developments and changes in the church's exegesis of Scripture. He gleaned this idea from his own doctoral work on Luther's interpretation of the Gospels and from his close reading of Luther's earliest interpretation of the Psalter.[2] Indeed, one could almost say that the history of Martin Luther and his early adherents is the history of their elucidation of Holy Writ, and that to appreciate best the differences between Luther and his late-medieval, Anabaptist, or Zwinglian opponents one could best examine their diverse interpretations of the Bible.

This book focuses on Martin Luther, Philip Melanchthon (his closest colleague at Wittenberg), and their followers and on the methods they used to unlock the meaning of the Bible for their age—but also for ours. As Ebeling himself discovered, Luther's approach to Scripture was so radically different from that of his late-medieval, scholastic contemporaries that it contained within it the seeds for the Reformation. One of the grounds for the ruptures in the sixteenth-century Western church arose out

---

1. Gerhard Ebeling, "Kirchengeschichte als Geschichte der Auslegung der Heiligen Schrift," in *Wort Gottes und Tradition* (Göttingen: Vandenhoeck & Ruprecht, 1964), 9–27.

2. Gerhard Ebeling, *Evangelische Evangeliumauslegung: Eine Untersuchung zu Luthers Hermeneutik* (Munich: Kaiser, 1942); Ebeling, "The Beginnings of Luther's Hermeneutics," *Lutheran Quarterly* 7 (1993): 129–58, 315–38, 451–68.

of various scholars' very different approaches to interpreting the Bible.

To be sure, Luther and his colleagues depended on a host of patristic and medieval biblical exegetes, as well as on the Renaissance scholarship of their own day, as will be investigated in chapter 1. But the way in which they combined these genuine insights into the Bible's meaning with their own readings resulted in a completely new and at the same time completely ancient way to approach the text.[3] Although later generations of exegetes often lost sight of the Wittenberg Reformers' unique contributions to biblical interpretation, the rediscovery of Reformation hermeneutics in the twentieth century led to a renewed respect for what they accomplished.

From the Renaissance debate over the relation between rhetoric and dialectics (logic), we glean in chapter 2 that both Luther and Melanchthon framed their approach to Scripture in terms of definition (what a thing is—the basis of dialectics) and effect (what a thing does—an interest of rhetoric). On the one hand, it meant that the Wittenberg exegetes took great stock in figuring out what the biblical text was actually saying. This implied both renewed interest in the nuance of words (e.g., the presence of Hebraisms in the Greek text [see the appendix]) and sensitivity to translation from the languages of the biblical author and into those of the later reader. But it also resulted in a new focus on the biblical author's own activity in shaping the text and, at the same time, a concern for the author's central point (described in the author's so-called *argumentum*). Philip Melanchthon went a step further and also organized the basic themes of all Scripture by employing *loci communes* (commonplaces), offering a Renaissance solution to the question of the Bible's unity.

On the other hand, asking about the text's effect on the hearer was never far removed from the work of interpretation. For the Reformers, the true meaning of the text could never be reduced to defining the text but always had to include how the text worked on its hearers and readers. Although the main harvest of

3. John O'Malley's analysis of Luther's preaching is very helpful in this regard. See his "Luther the Preacher," in *The Martin Luther Quincentennial*, ed. Gerhard Dünnhaupt (Detroit: Wayne State University Press, 1985), 3–16.

this approach is the topic in chapter 3, chapter 2 examines several other important results of this interest. Focusing on the effect implied for Luther a single-minded interest in *Was Christum treibet*—what pushes, fixes on, or emphasizes Christ. The point of exegesis is to lead interpreter and hearer into relation with Christ, the savior of the world. This approach led to Luther's skepticism about James. But Luther and his colleagues at Wittenberg also understood the divine biblical authorship from a particular point of view—not simply asserting Scripture's inspiration but emphasizing its profitability (see 2 Tim 3:16). The emphasis on effect also allowed Luther to understand meaning in close relation to experience. In Luther's case it meant using and transforming certain aspects of the monastic *lectio divina* to serve his work. Again, Luther's unique view of the theologian as operating under the shadow of the cross's foolishness led him to view Scripture as counter-rational—destroying the wisdom of the world and its philosophers with God's foolish wisdom.

The heart of Wittenberg's exegetical proposal to the church catholic regarding the text's effect on the hearer—the distinction between law and gospel—is the theme of chapter 3. This distinction began for Luther as a reflection on 2 Corinthians 3:6, "The letter kills, but the Spirit gives life," seen through the lens of Augustine's tract *On the Spirit and the Letter*. God uses the law to reveal the truth of the human condition (sin), to terrify, and to put to death the old creature. At the same time, the gospel reveals the truth of God's mercy in Christ (forgiveness), comforts, and brings to life the person of faith. Yet God also uses the law in this world, separate and apart from the gospel, to keep order and restrain evil. When in 1534 Melanchthon conceives a "third use" of the law, he intended it to reject both antinomian tendencies among some of Luther's followers and the mixing of God's law with the gospel as proposed by some adherents of the old theology.

How might this concatenation of approaches to the sacred text still find use today? To address that question, chapters 4 and 5 look at two kinds of texts: the "last words" of Jesus (chap. 4) and selections from the Psalter (chap. 5). By placing the author's own reflections on these texts side by side with Luther's, readers can judge for themselves how this five-hundred-year-old tradition may still help hearers experience the text in the present by unlocking the meaning of the biblical text—both its definition and its effect—for today.

Special thanks to Mark Powell for encouraging me to write this volume, and for the careful editing of Scott Tunseth and Beth Ann Gaede, who made the book far more readable. A special word of thanks to my friend Irving Sandberg, one of the church's best and most faithful preachers, for reading the manuscript. The errors and shortcomings, of course, are all mine. I dedicate this book to all of my former and future students, with the admonition that they preach the "blessed" gospel.

Timothy J. Wengert
Riverton, New Jersey
Feast of Sts. Philip and James, 2018

1.

The Cloud of Witnesses

In 1513, Martin Luther entered the University of Wittenberg's lecture hall for the first time as *doctor ecclesiae*, teacher of the church, and began his career with biblical lectures on the psalms, now known as the *Dictata super Psalterium*.[1] He followed the lecture style of his scholastic teachers in Erfurt: providing both short glosses on each psalm and longer comments, called *scholia*, on verses of particular interest to him. These earliest lectures on the psalms help fix Luther's place in the history of biblical interpretation as he showed what he inherited from past models of exegesis and what he learned from new methods developing in the Renaissance. Without this background, one can measure Luther's unique contributions to biblical interpretation only with difficulty.

THE PATRISTIC, MEDIEVAL, AND RENAISSANCE BACKGROUND

Literal and Spiritual Meanings: The Quadriga

In his first lecture, Martin Luther presented the traditional framework for biblical interpretation, introducing his students

---

1. LW 10–11 (WA 3, 4, and 55/1–2).

to the medieval *Quadriga*, a fourfold interpretive schema consisting of one literal meaning and three spiritual meanings. If the word in the text were "Mt. Zion," for example, it contained four possible fields of meaning: first (literally) as a place in Palestine; second (allegorically)[2] as the church; third (tropologically) as the elect soul; and fourth (anagogically) as heaven and all the saints. To be sure, in order to set proper boundaries for the three spiritual interpretations, students were reminded that any spiritual truth uncovered by this method had to be supported by a literal passage somewhere else in Scripture. These spiritual meanings were governed by three passive gerunds summarizing the three "theological virtues": *credenda* (what must be believed, i.e., faith) for allegory, *agenda* (what must be done, i.e., love) for tropology, and *speranda* (what must be hoped for, i.e., hope) for anagogy.

One prooftext for this method of interpreting Scripture was 2 Corinthians 3:6: "The letter kills, but the Spirit gives life." Each interpreter was obliged to move beyond the literal, historical meanings of texts (which killed) to discover the deeper, hidden spiritual meanings (which gave life). This approach to the biblical text reaches all the way back into the patristic period, when one of the first great Christian exegetes, Origen of Alexandria, took over a Platonic method of interpreting the Greek classics that the famous Jewish exegete Philo of Alexandria had already used on the Hebrew Scriptures. Origen argued that there were three levels of biblical interpretation corresponding to three different kinds of Christians.[3] For the *hylic* believers, simple people embedded in the material world (from the Greek: ὕλη), there were the literal stories. For the *psychikoi*, those whose souls (from the Greek: ψυχή) yearn for the Good, there was the moral content of Scripture. For the *pneumatikoi*, the truly spiritual ones (from the Greek: πνεῦμα), there were deeper, spiritual meanings hidden within the text.

This approach found its way into the Western tradition both directly, through translations of Origen's work into Latin, and

2. This technical use of the term *allegory* refers always to doctrine involving the relation of Christ and the church. Modern English uses the term much more broadly for all forms of spiritual interpretation of a text.

3. Origen of Alexandria, *On First Principles* [*De principiis*], trans. G. W. Butterworth (Gloucester, MA: Peter Smith, 1973), 4.2.4.

indirectly, through Ambrose, bishop of Milan, and from him to Augustine, bishop of Hippo in North Africa. When it came to the Psalter, no interpretation garnered more influence in the West than Augustine's *Expositions on the Psalms*, a work on which later interpreters, including Luther, depended for their own work. By the time of Augustine, the strict division among listeners defined by Origen had weakened, as Christians became more and more accustomed to spiritual interpretations of texts. One constant, however, was the conviction that all Scripture should edify its readers or, as 2 Timothy 3:16 insists in the King James Version, be "profitable." The Quadriga and other schemes for discovering the spiritual meanings of sacred texts allowed the preacher to take passages of questionable value or complete obscurity and find deeper meaning within them. Based on broader suggestions from Augustine, Psalm 137's repulsive desire to smash Babylonian babies against rocks could come to mean celibate priests smashing incipient, lustful thoughts against the Rock, which is Christ.[4]

Christological Exegesis

Luther also included a second set of prefatory remarks for the printed copies of Psalms that his students used to insert their teacher's remarks.[5] He insisted—as had the earlier exegetical tradition in the West going back at least to Cassiodorus and, before him, to Augustine and suggested by the New Testament itself—that Christ was the speaker of each psalm. Nicholas of Lyra, in his introduction to the Psalter, used Aristotle's four causes to distinguish the efficient causes of the psalms (princi-

4. Augustine, *Expositions on the Book of Psalms*, Psalm 137, par. 12, in *A Select Library of Nicene and Post-Nicene Fathers of the Christian Church*, ed. Philip Schaff (1886–1889, repr., Grand Rapids: Eerdmans, 1974), series 1, 8:632. Augustine applied this text to all Christians battling lustful thoughts. After giving a literal interpretation, even Nicholas of Lyra notes that the moral meaning could have to do with the penitents who mourn their sin and captivity under demons, upon which they pray God's punishment. The Roman Confutation of the Augsburg Confession in 1530 used similar interpretation to support the celibate priesthood. See Robert Kolb et al., *Sources and Contexts of the Book of Concord* (Minneapolis: Fortress Press, 2001), 126.

5. LW 10:3–7.

pally God; instrumentally David and other authors) from the material cause, which is Christ, in the mode of divine praise.[6] Perhaps echoing Lyra's comments, Luther labeled his introduction the "Preface of Jesus Christ" for his first students, insisting that the Psalter actually described Christ's life, death, and resurrection. Such an approach was a combination of allegory (technically speaking, the conversation between Christ and the church) and typology—the insistence that actions described in the Old Testament, such as the sacrifice of Isaac in Genesis 22, foreshadowed an action of Christ in the New, in this case his sacrificial death in humanity's stead.

That the ancient and medieval church employed both the Quadriga and typology in their interpretations of Scripture did not represent an abandonment of biblical truth but an acceptance of methods found in Scripture itself, especially the New Testament. In Galatians 4:24 Paul describes his use of the slave woman and free woman in Genesis as figurative (Greek: ἀλληγορούμενα, from which we derive the word *allegory*). Or again, in 1 Corinthians 10:4, we learn that the rock from which the Israelites drank was Christ. In Romans 5:14, Paul calls Adam a type (Greek: τύπος) of Christ. In medieval exegesis, theologians worked to accommodate all these meanings to the literal sense of Scripture.

In the late Middle Ages, a way of doing theology developed in German-speaking lands, usually labeled by scholars German mysticism and including works by Johannes Tauler and the anonymous author of the *Theologia Deutsch*.[7] Johann von Staupitz, Luther's mentor and the head of the Augustinian order in Germany, to which Luther belonged, is sometimes also included in this group. Although Luther himself would not have recognized the designation of mysticism—medieval theol-

---

6. Nicholas of Lyra, *Biblia cum Postilla litteralis*, 4 vols. (Lyon, ca. 1485), 2:Mm 1r. The formal cause is the division of the book and its praise of the mind ascending to heaven, and the final cause is for believers' use and salvation.

7. See Volker Leppin and Berndt Hamm, eds., *Gottes Nähe unmittelbar erfahren: Mystik im Mittelalter und bei Martin Luther* (Tübingen: Mohr Siebeck, 2007). It might be better to understand these authors as deeply pastoral in their approach to theology and exegesis rather than committed to a kind of spirituality that Luther would later criticize. They were theologians of the heart. See Scott Hendrix, "Martin Luther's Reformation of Spirituality," *Lutheran Quarterly* 13 (1999): 249–70.

ogy was far broader and less well defined than scholars often imagine—he did recognize the uniqueness of these thinkers, who played an important role in his developing theology especially between 1517 and 1520, when he published two versions of the *Theologia Deutsch*, praised von Staupitz for having aided him, and championed Tauler as a premier theologian, despite (or because of!) the fact that he wrote exclusively in German.[8] These thinkers, especially Tauler, provided Luther with a way of incorporating the paradoxes and reversals in Scripture into his theology, and thus a way of understanding Scripture that had direct consequences for the hearer, called human logic and reason into question, and drove a hearer to trust in the God who comes in the dust. As we will see, this approach to theology, labeled by Luther the theology of the cross, had far-reaching effects for his Christocentric interpretation of the Bible.

The Literal Meaning(s) of Texts

The interest in spiritual or typological meanings should not cloud the fact that ancient and medieval interpreters also cared deeply about the literal, historical meaning of Scripture. In the ancient church there was often discussion of the facts surrounding a particular biblical event. Unlike Gnostics, who saw the literal meaning of the Old Testament tied to an ignorant, lesser divine being, orthodox Christians insisted that the literal text of the entire Bible was capable of edifying the listener. Moreover, texts like the Pauline Epistles required interpretation of the actual arguments Paul was making in the text. Especially the Epistles were expected to inform readers directly and literally. They provided roadmaps for interpreting other parts of Scripture.

In the early Middle Ages, the so-called Victorines also focused their interpretation of Scripture on the letter and its history.[9] But scholastic interpreters by no means denigrated the literal

8. Martin Brecht, *Martin Luther: His Road to Reformation, 1483–1521*, trans. James L. Schaaf (Philadelphia: Fortress Press, 1985), 137–44.

9. Beryl Smalley, *The Study of the Bible in the Middle Ages* (Oxford: Blackwell, 1952).

text in search of moral and spiritual meaning. Thomas Aquinas, for example, insisted on the priority of the literal meaning of texts. Several generations later, Nicholas of Lyra put even more emphasis on the historical-literal text, returning to the Hebrew original and relying on rabbinic sources to help understand difficult Hebrew passages. Although never a strict follower of Lyra's work, Luther did find plenty of help from that medieval exegete, whose interpretation of the entire Bible was widely available in print at the end of the Middle Ages. A Latin couplet, composed after Luther's death, insisted that "si Lyra non lyrasset, Luther non saltasset" (if Lyra had not played the lyre, Luther would not have danced). Although this verse exaggerates the connection, it does underscore Luther's openness to using ancient and medieval sources to interpret Scripture. Indeed, early Lutheran biblical scholars (like those of any age) were always in conversation with their predecessors.[10] Whatever theological and institutional breaks define the relation between Wittenberg and Rome, the strongest continuity arises from their sources for biblical interpretation. Only much more recently in the history of the church have certain forms of biblical interpretation become tradition-denying and thus more dependent on novelty than continuity with past exegetes.

But Aquinas and Lyra also developed a more complicated view of the literal meaning of a text. Under most circumstances, only words (*verba*) signified things (*res*). But reading certain Old Testament practices and events as types of Christ meant that things could also represent other things (the temple sacrifices as a type of Christ's sacrifice, circumcision as a type of baptism, the exodus as a type of Christ's death and resurrection, etc.). This opened up a second level of literal meaning, namely, the prophetic-literal meaning. In the first instance, this second literal meaning was seen as derivative and helpful in distinguishing typology from other forms of spiritual exegesis. In Lyra's case, it seems to have given him permission to concentrate on the literal texts of the Hebrew Scriptures, although as a Franciscan he was

---

10. Timothy J. Wengert, *Philip Melanchthon's "Annotationes in Johannem" of 1523 in Relation to Its Predecessors and Contemporaries* (Geneva: Droz, 1987).

not uninterested in the moral nuggets found in the text and provided a separate collection of those insights.

In the early sixteenth century, however, a French humanist interpreter of the psalms, Jacques Lefèvre d'Étaples, defined the historical-literal text as a "killing letter" and saw the exegete's task to escape it and to focus instead on the prophetic-literal meaning. Luther's use of Lefèvre in his first Psalms lectures resulted in his distinguishing these two levels of literal meaning and consistently giving preference to the prophetic, as his "Preface of Jesus Christ" made clear.[11] By the time he lectured on Psalms for a second time, from 1519 to 1521, however, Luther's view had changed dramatically, as he focused on the simple, literal (i.e., historical) meaning of the text and assumed that that meaning had direct application to the believer's life.

Humanist Methods

Another major component of Luther's approach to the Bible came from his immediate surroundings and a movement that came to be known as Renaissance humanism. In the twentieth century scholars struggled with definitions of humanism, often viewing it as a precursor to the eighteenth-century Enlightenment and rationalism. Moreover, given that Martin Luther engaged in a famous debate over human choice in matters of salvation with the prince of humanists north of the Alps, Erasmus of Rotterdam, it was easy to pit humanism against Luther and Lutheranism. Such a narrow view of this movement has meant that many scholars have overlooked Luther's indebtedness to it and, at the same time, struggled to understand how some of Luther's most well-known supporters, such as Philip Melanchthon and Justus Jonas, could so clearly employ humanism's methods to interpret texts.[12]

Today, scholars overcome this myopic view of humanism in

11. Jacques Lefèvre d'Étaples, *Qvincvplex Psalterium, Gallicum, Romanum, Hebraicum, Vetus, Conciliatum* (Paris: H. Stephan, 1509).

12. Timothy J. Wengert and M. Patrick Graham, eds., *Philip Melanchthon (1497–1560) and the Commentary* (Sheffield: Sheffield Academic, 1997); and Irene Dingel, ed., *Justus Jonas (1493–1555) und seine Bedeutung für die Wittenberger Reformation* (Leipzig: Evangelische Verlagsanstalt, 2009).

two ways. First, the more that is known about sixteenth-century university life north of the Alps, the more it becomes clear that Erasmus was not the be-all and end-all of the movement, so that his debate with Luther over bound choice has nothing to do directly with Luther's debt to humanism and its methods. Second, more pragmatic ways to define humanism have allowed researchers to focus more accurately on its method, held in common by all humanists, and separate it from particular viewpoints on specific theological or philosophical topics. No one helped this shift more than Paul Oskar Kristeller, a refugee from Nazi Germany who taught at Columbia University for years and studied Italian humanism. Kristeller noted that while the word *humanism* stems from nineteenth-century descriptions of the Renaissance, the word *'umaniste* was long used by students at Italian universities during the Renaissance to describe teachers and tutors on the edges of university life who taught such things as rhetoric, moral philosophy, history, and (with the influx of Greek-speaking scholars to the Italian peninsula after the fall of Constantinople in 1453) classical Greek.[13]

Two slogans defined humanists' common interests: *bonae literae* (good letters) and *ad fontes* ([returning] to the [purest] springs). Around the first, *bonae literae*, humanists developed a program for purifying the Latin language from medieval neologisms, developing classical styles as defined by Cicero and Quintilian, and reading and imitating the very best literature from the past. Some took this task so seriously that they tried to write and speak Latin exactly as Cicero had, searching for classical expressions to replace the many Greek loanwords that had crept into ecclesiastical Latin (such as *ecclesia* [church] or *episkopos* [bishop]). (Erasmus even mocked these strict "Ciceronians" in a sarcastic tract titled *Ciceronianus*.[14]) Humanists also looked with disdain on scholastic theology, criticizing its dependence on dialectics (logic), its ignorance of rhetoric, and its many neologisms.

13. Paul Oskar Kristeller, *Renaissance Thought and Its Sources*, ed. Michael Mooney (New York: Columbia University Press, 1979).

14. See Erasmus of Rotterdam, *Ciceronianus*, in *Ausgewählte Schriften*, ed. Werner Welzig (Darmstadt: Wissenschaftliche Buchgesellschaft, 1968-72), 7:1–355.

Around the second, *ad fontes*, humanists scoured European libraries looking for and publishing ancient classical texts using the new invention of the printing press. They also employed their considerable textual expertise to determine whether such texts were genuine and to purge from them later accretions. North of the Alps, this return to the most ancient sources included a renewed interest in the church fathers. In this interest Erasmus excelled, publishing through the offices of the renowned Basel printer Johannes Froben new editions of Augustine, Jerome, and others. He is best known, however, for producing the first Greek New Testament in 1516, which came out only slightly before a similar project in Spain headed up by Cardinal Ximenes. In 1516, Erasmus's *Novum Instrumentum*, as he titled it, presented in parallel columns the Greek text and the standard Latin translation, the Vulgate. In a separate volume of notes, the *Annotationes in Novum Instrumentum*, Erasmus provided specific criticisms of the Vulgate and suggestions for improvement. Here he joined other humanist interpreters, including Lorenzo Valla and Lefèvre, who also proposed corrections to the standard text. In the second edition of 1519 (now renamed the *Novum Testamentum*), however, Erasmus replaced the Vulgate with his own Latin translation. This meant that from the second edition on, the *Annotationes* became more and more a defense of his own translation rather than simply suggestions for changes of the Vulgate.

Humanism's core commitments to good letters and pure sources opened up a different way of reading Scripture. While exegetes in the ancient church, such as Augustine and Chrysostom, often went verse by verse through a biblical text, they and their scholastic descendants could also view texts quite apart from the human authors and any overarching themes that these authors may have had in mind. Humanists, on the contrary, could view texts more holistically, as the product of actual writers and speakers. One could legitimately ask what the overall point was, rather than become submerged in only a quest for the meaning of words and phrases. The humanist interest in rhetoric also meant that exegetes could focus more on the structure of texts and their emotional impact on the reader. At the same time, with a renewed interest in the original languages (first Greek and later also Hebrew), Renaissance interpreters could focus on sacred texts freed from the filter of the Latin Vulgate. All of these matters became of great interest to Luther and his colleagues in Wittenberg. Indeed, using Kristeller's definition, we can say that Luther himself was a humanist and that the University of Wittenberg under his influence (among others) was becoming an important center of humanist interpretation of Scripture even before the Reformation began.[15]

LUTHER'S CONTRIBUTIONS TO THE EXEGETICAL METHOD

All well and good. The first thing to remember is that Luther was indeed dependent on the fifteen hundred years of Christian biblical interpretation that preceded him. He knew and respected it; he used its results and insights throughout his life. This contrasts with the tradition-denying stance of many modern interpreters who have constructed a wall between their "critical" work and the past. But, at the same time, Luther's early lectures on Psalms, followed quickly by lectures on Romans, Galatians, and Hebrews, also demonstrate that something quite profound was occurring in Luther's interpretation of the Bible.[16]

From "Letter and Spirit" to "Law and Gospel"

For one thing, after describing the Quadriga, Luther immediately turned it into an "Octriga," so to speak, dividing each of the four traditional meanings into two: the killing letter and the life-giving Spirit. Thus any term in Scripture could, on

15. Helmar Junghans, *Der junge Luther und die Humanisten* (Weimar: Böhlau, 1984); Birgit Stolt, *Martin Luthers Rhetorik des Herzens* (Tübingen: Mohr Siebeck, 2000); and Carl P. E. Springer, *Cicero in Heaven: The Roman Rhetor and Luther's Reformation* (Leiden: Brill, 2018).

16. Gerhard Ebeling, "The Beginnings of Luther's Hermeneutics," *Lutheran Quarterly* 7 (1993): 129–58, 315–38, 451–68; Berndt Hamm, *The Early Luther: Stages in a Reformation Reorientation*, trans. Martin Lohrmann (Grand Rapids: Eerdmans, 2014); Kenneth Hagen, *Luther's Approach to Scripture as Seen in His "Commentaries" on Galatians 1519–1538* (Tübingen: Mohr Siebeck, 1993).

a literal, allegorical, tropological, or anagogical level, cut two ways: as a word that condemned sin and a word that gave life to the redeemed. In this way, Luther was reviving an often-neglected, secondary interpretation of 2 Corinthians 3:6 also found in Augustine.[17] In the old bishop's *On Christian Doctrine*, we discover the "Rules of Tychonius," seven interpretive turns proposed by the moderate Donatist thinker Tychonius, the third of which distinguished commands from promises. And Augustine, in his interpretation of Romans, *On the Spirit and the Letter*, went to great lengths to distinguish commands and promises as well. But Luther's own approach reinforced another neglected aspect of biblical interpretation: that the Scripture works on its hearers, putting to death and bringing to life.

But what is that life? Here, in another deviation from the standard methods, Luther changed the tropological interpretation to focus not so much on love (as demanded in the Quadriga) but, as he said, "on the righteousness of faith." Was Luther abandoning traditional spiritual interpretations? Not really, since he continued to provide spiritual interpretations for texts, especially parables, throughout his teaching career. But he surely had reframed the interpreter's task, no longer asking, What is this text telling me to believe, do, or hope for and how do I get this from the text? but rather, What is this text doing to me? How is it putting me to death and bringing me to life, that is, declaring me righteous?

From Christocentric Exegesis to the Cries of the Faithful

For another thing, although Luther continued to read Old Testament texts christologically, he nevertheless also discovered another voice in the psalms, what one scholar has called "the faithful synagogue."[18] Suddenly, Luther radically simplified the interpreter's task. Instead of asking, first, how are these words

17. Augustine, *On Christian Doctrine*, 3.30.42–3.37.56, trans. D. W. Robertson (Indianapolis: Liberal Arts Press, 1958), 104–17; Augustine, *On the Spirit and the Letter*, in *A Select Library of Nicene and Post-Nicene Fathers of the Christian Church*, ed. Philip Schaff (Reprint: Grand Rapids: Eerdmans, 1974), series 1, 5:83–114.

18. James Samuel Preus, *From Shadow to Promise: Old Testament Interpretations from Augustine to the Young Luther* (Cambridge, MA: Harvard University Press, 1969).

Christ's words and, second, how does his life apply to mine, Luther now discovered that Old Testament believers in God spoke words to God and about God—words that reflect the interpreter's own needs and life in Christ. When, ten years after those first Psalms lectures, Luther wrote a preface to his German translation of the Psalter, it was the cries of the saints that he most clearly heard.[19]

At the same time, and under the influence of German mysticism, Luther developed his theology of the cross—not a theory about the cross regarding the atonement but "the revelation of God under the appearance of the opposite."[20] This meant that every time Luther saw a text that contradicted human reason, he immediately assumed that it was attacking humanity's rational hubris and providing a way to look at Scripture and thus God's heart that directly contradicted and, indeed, destroyed rational explanations of how God ought to act. Thus Christ continued to stand at the heart of the biblical text but hidden under the appearance of the opposite, that is, in the last place one would reasonably look.

Luther the Humanist

Luther's humanism reveals itself in several aspects of his biblical interpretation. Not only did he rediscover the lively and life-giving history of the text in the faithful synagogue, but he also showed profound interest in the effect of the biblical text on the reader and hearer, one of Renaissance humanism's greatest concerns for all literature. In addition, from the very beginning of his career as a teacher of the church, Luther showed a profound interest in the original languages of the text. In the case of Hebrew, we know that already in the lectures on the psalms Luther was familiar with the work by Johannes Reuchlin on the

19. See below, chap. 5, pp. 128–32.
20. As he wrote against Erasmus in *On the Bound Will* (WA 18:633; LW 33:62), explaining 1 Sam 2:6), "Non autem remotius absconduntur, quam sub contrario obiectu, sensu, experientia" (It [everything which is believed] cannot, however, be more deeply hidden than under an object, perception, or experience which is contrary to it).

Hebrew text of the penitential psalms and that he was teaching himself Hebrew.

In the case of Greek, Luther's Romans lectures prove that as soon as Erasmus's Greek text was available, Luther procured a copy and began teaching himself Greek and using Erasmus's *Annotationes* on the text.[21] Moreover, he was sufficiently confident in his own interpretation of Romans and Galatians that he even disagreed with the Dutchman on his approach to Paul's letters, which Luther gleaned especially from Erasmus's prefaces to the books of the New Testament and from his sophisticated paraphrases of Paul's letters also published at this time.

Luther's Legacy

In combination with these interests, Luther and his colleagues in Wittenberg began to develop their own unique approach to Scripture, which will be the topic of the following chapters. First, the Wittenberg exegetes, for all their concern for the meaning of the words, the literary style, and the historical context, did not limit the meaning of the text to these things. Instead, they universally assumed that meaning encompasses two things: the historical and literary definition of a text *and* its effect on the readers and hearers. In so doing, they took the very different interests of dialectics (logic) and rhetoric and bound them together. While grammar and logic could determine what the biblical text was saying, rhetoric always inquired after the effect of that written or spoken text on its readers and hearers. Only in combination could an exegete uncover a biblical passage's true meaning.

Second, because Wittenberg's exegetes believed the meaning of a text combines both definition and effect, they always viewed Scripture in terms of what they called "law and gospel." For them, the law always accuses—not just as a statement of fact but also as a description of effect, where accusation always brings about guilt, terror, and death. At the same time, the gospel always forgives the guilty, comforts the terrified, and brings to life those dead in unbelief by making them believers. From

21. LW 25 (WA 56/1).

this perspective, the Holy Spirit is always working through the Word of God to make believers.

Of course, third, the exegetes' understanding that the goal of the text is faith did not undermine for them the importance of figuring out what the biblical text actually says. Here, a host of humanist techniques for interpreting ancient text came into play. Greek and Hebrew became irreplaceable tools for the exegete. Understanding both the logic and the rhetoric of the biblical authors allowed new insights into the text, as exegetes investigated the overarching unity of literary documents rather than succumbing to the temptation to reduce the Bible to a golden chain of unrelated moral or doctrinal nuggets. Knowledge of history also helped place the texts into their proper contexts. The more one knew about Israel and the early church, the better one was equipped to understand Scripture.

This approach guaranteed that Wittenberg's exegetes would also be looking for the center of a biblical book and interpreting texts not slavishly, verse by verse, but dynamically through the author's own field of meaning. It is no accident that Philip Melanchthon was the first exegete who provided a rhetorical outline of Romans or that his and Luther's student Caspar Cruciger Sr. was the first to argue that John 20:30–31 revealed John's intent for his entire Gospel. Nor is it surprising that Luther and Melanchthon insisted that Romans provided the center of the entire Scripture, without which interpretation always devolved into legalism.

Fourth, one way that Wittenberg theologians uncovered the effect of the biblical text was by appreciating how it attacked human logic. While "theologians of glory," as Luther nicknamed them in his *Heidelberg Disputation*, sought out what is strong and (thus) logical, the theologian of the cross found God working in the last place anyone would reasonably look: on the cross, in weakness and foolishness. This view calls into question a certain penchant among later Protestant theologians to define Scripture's inspiration in terms of its strength (unfailing and inerrant). Instead, the Scripture works as Word of God in the weakness and foolishness of the cross by working Christ's death and resurrection on the hearer, putting to death and bringing to life, destroying unbelief and creating faith, that is, doing an alien work before doing its proper work.

This theology also sheds light on Wittenbergers' insistence that justification by faith alone implies understanding the righteousness of faith as a Hebraism, depicting what happens *in foro*, that is, in a court where the convicted sinner is declared, simply declared, righteous—not on the basis of any merit or worthiness but strictly from the mercy of God.[22] This declaring sinners to be what they are not (namely, righteous) is itself contrarational, indeed, contradictory to all Aristotelian and Ciceronian definitions of righteousness that insisted on giving "to each his [or her] own." To be sure, the believing sinner gives to God what belongs to God by confessing God to be righteous in judgment, but at the same time sinners receive what properly speaking could never be their own. Rather than basing justification on the *logic* of the courtroom, the Wittenberg exegetes insist on true illogic. The judge "breaks the law" by upsetting the "just" order of things and establishing a justice based on mercy—itself a foolish contradiction of humanity's reasonable view of righteousness. In this very act, the accusing law comes to its proper end, and the sinner is clothed in Christ's righteousness. Only when theologians replace the foolishness of this declaration with the inner logic of making someone pay to balance justice and mercy do forensic justification and the imputation of an alien righteousness revert to a theology of glory and, in Wittenberg's eyes, undermine the very heart of the gospel and its proper interpretation.

22. See the appendix.

2.

Not "Just the Facts, Ma'am": From Definition to Effect

The classic television show from the 1950s and 1960s *Dragnet* often had its hero, Sergeant Joe Friday of the Los Angeles Police Department, interview a victim or witness by beginning, "Just the facts, Ma'am." This positive, modern approach to facts and events has had an enormous impact on how we view the world. Despite the overwhelming complexity of particle physics and Heisenberg's uncertainty principle—to say nothing of quarks and dark matter and black holes—we still navigate our universe on the basis of the "sure" facts of Newtonian physics. The same goes for biblical studies—liberal or conservative—where the search for the single meaning and intent of the authors (or Author) has dominated approaches to Scripture for the past 150 years or more. Even "postmodern" attempts to come to terms with the relative nature of reading a text for truth (putting it more squarely in the mind and experience of the beholder or exegete) still claim assurance about one fact: that we all have our own, albeit personal approaches to texts and to truth. By contrast, Wittenberg's interpreters insisted that the actual, concrete meaning of a text always involved discovering two interrelated things: the definition of a text and its effect on the hearers. That is, true interpretation of the Bible always involves more than "just the facts" and includes what those "facts" are doing to us as we read them.

This twofold approach allows us to take seriously past interpreters of Scripture rather than imagine that it is up to us alone to figure out what a biblical author was trying to say. Part of the reason that earlier exegetes of Scripture may seem so far removed from today's concerns and, thus, out of date arises from our modern (or postmodern) hubris about the nature of the facts in the text. Luther and Melanchthon—to say nothing of Thomas Aquinas, Augustine, or Jerome—may often seem to our eyes to confuse what the text means with what it meant to them, or else they seem to confuse grinding their own theological axes with the text's meaning, thus proving the postmodern skeptic right. A careful reading of the history of biblical interpretation, however, actually leads to the opposite view: that the Bible has a rather limited field of meanings and that many of today's debates may already be lurking in the past—even when present-day exegetes have no clue of their participation in such earlier conversations.[1] Moreover, precritical readers have an advantage over our own rationally inclined approaches to the Bible: they assume (albeit naively) that the Bible has meaning not just for the past but also for the present and that that meaning more or less becomes clear when the text addresses the reader. This assumption is shared by the biblical authors themselves, who rarely if ever wrote only for themselves or an "immediate" audience but almost always had a much wider set of readers in mind. They assumed that what they had to say would outlive them.

Nowhere is this assumption of a wider audience more graphically displayed than in the woodcuts designed for the Luther Bible, first published in 1534. Although in the early books of the Old Testament the illustrators stuck with medieval precedent, their pictures for each prophet were unique.[2] With few exceptions, the prophet, often clothed in sixteenth-century peasant dress, was always depicted in the foreground preaching to

1. David C. Steinmetz, "The Superiority of Pre-Critical Exegesis," *Theology Today* 27 (1980): 27–38.

2. Philipp Schmidt, *Die Illustration der Lutherbibel 1522–1700: Ein Stück abendländische Kultur- und Kirchengeschichte mit Verzeichnissen der Bibeln, Bilder und Künstler* (Basel: Reinhardt, 1962).

his own people (who in one case even turn away and cover their ears). In the background, the artists illustrated some typological connection to an event in Jesus's life referred to in New Testament. Thus, for example, Hosea shows the resurrection; Isaiah, the crucifixion; Zechariah, the entry into Jerusalem; Joel, Peter preaching at Pentecost. The woodcut for Joel is particularly interesting, since it shows two acts of preaching (by Joel and Peter) in the same place (Jerusalem, shown as a prosperous German city square) and, thus, two sets of hearers. This forthright approach to the prophet's calling to preach to his own people disappears a hundred years later in the famous illustrations of the Merian Bible. In them the prophet, no longer in sixteenth-century dress, stands alone in a barren landscape with only the typological reference depicted behind him. For example, Micah, standing in an empty foreground, prophesies the birth of Jesus in Bethlehem, depicted in the distance. But to paraphrase the famous example ascribed to George Berkeley, if a prophet proclaims in an empty wilderness, is it really proclamation? Who's listening? Wittenberg exegesis rested on the conviction that the text's meaning depends on its being heard and believed.

THE FACTS

Martin Luther and Philip Melanchthon, along with a host of Wittenberg exegetes who followed in their footsteps, were children of the Renaissance. That is, they benefited from the shift in interpretation (often labeled humanism), that is, an insistence on returning to the oldest and best sources (in theology this meant to the church fathers and the original texts of Scripture) and a deep commitment to using the very best language Greek and Roman literature had to offer. This led them to develop highly sophisticated approaches to the biblical text. They recognized figures of speech and patterns of language in their authors. They used rhetorical tools to outline texts (especially the Pauline corpus) and to appreciate a biblical author's attempts to move the hearer. They assumed that the more one knew Hebrew, Aramaic, and Greek, the better one could understand Scripture. And they turned a Renaissance debate over the relation of rhetoric and dialectics (logic) to their advantage in rediscovering that a text's actual meaning included more than simply definition (the facts) but had to take account of its use and goal by the author and the church (the effect).

Plumbing the Text

Until quite recently, the churches of the Reformation have uniformly insisted that their ministers acquire some knowledge of Greek and Hebrew in order to divine the precise meaning of Scripture. Luther admits that while it is possible for a preacher lacking such knowledge to succeed, he assumes that their sermons will inevitably fall flat.[3] It is hard for us to comprehend what an impact learning these languages had on the scholars in early modern Europe. Perhaps our own reactions to seeing the backside of the moon or pictures of Pluto up close or viewing the latest skeletons harvested from Olduvai Gorge, or the Dead Sea Scrolls, might come close to the wonder and otherworldliness these new, old languages evoked; but these things fall far short of the impact of reading God's Word in its original tongues.

The desire to master these languages must have been overwhelming, as Luther's own biography demonstrates. In 1516, as soon as Erasmus's *Novum Instrumentum* with its parallel columns of the Greek and the standard Latin (Vulgate) texts started rolling off the presses of the Basel printer Johannes Froben, Luther got hold of a copy and began to teach himself enough of the language to use it in the classroom. Of course, he was helped enormously by Erasmus's annotations on the Greek text, which for the first edition (also published in 1516) pointed out places where the Vulgate needed improvement, while at the same time criticizing scholastic theologians' poor use of Scripture. Erasmus's *Annotations* not only gave Luther a leg up in translating the Greek, but it also contained countless references to the church fathers, which Luther also eagerly used.[4]

---

3. Martin Luther, *To the Councilmen of All Cities in Germany That They Establish and Maintain Christian Schools* (1524), LW 45:365 (WA 15:42).

4. A particularly good example of this comes with his comments several years later

Luther's personal commitment to the original text of Scripture had already shown up in his work on the psalms, where in his first lectures he employed the work of Johannes Reuchlin on the penitential psalms as well as comments on the Hebrew text found in the works of Jacques Lefèvre d'Étaples and Nicholas of Lyra. It is no accident that his very first publication, which appeared in early 1517, was a German translation of and commentary on the penitential psalms, squarely based on his reading of Reuchlin. His knowledge of Hebrew increased slowly over the next decade, as Siegfried Räder has painstakingly demonstrated.[5] As the biblical lectures became the heart of Wittenberg's theological curriculum, Luther more and more concentrated on the Hebrew Scripture, while still occasionally lecturing on New Testament texts.[6] In addition, he relied on his knowledge of Hebrew for the Wittenberg translation of the Old Testament and revisions, which stretched from 1523 to 1545.

But Luther's commitment to the original languages had immediate effects on Wittenberg's curriculum too. In 1517–1518, the humanist-oriented faculty set out to find teachers for Greek and Hebrew. Although a permanent Hebrew teacher was not found until the 1520s, when Matthäus Aurogallus came to the faculty, Wittenberg had much better success finding a Greek teacher, calling (upon the recommendation of Reuchlin) the twenty-one-year-old Philip Melanchthon to the newly created post in the arts faculty. The inaugural address

on Heb 11:1, where instead of understanding the word *substantia* ontologically (i.e., faith as the being of things hoped for) Luther followed Jerome in arguing for the standard usage of the word in Greek as possession (as in English one can talk about a "man of substance," i.e., a rich man). See Luther's lectures on Hebrews (1517–1518), LW 29:229–31 (WA 57/3:226–29). For his use of Erasmus in the Ninety-Five Theses, see Timothy J. Wengert, "The 95 Theses as Luther's Template for Reading Scripture," *Lutheran Quarterly* 31 (2017): 249–66.

5. Siegfried Räder, *Das Hebräische bei Luther untersucht bis zum Ende der ersten Psalmenvorlesung* (Tübingen: Mohr Siebeck, 1961); Räder, *Die Benutzung des masoretischen Textes bei Luther in der Zeit zwischen der ersten und zweiten Psalmenvorlesung (1515–1518)* (Tübingen: Mohr Siebeck, 1966); Räder, *Grammatica Theologica: Studien zu Luthers "Operationes in Psalmos"* (Tübingen: Mohr Siebeck, 1977).

6. In the late 1520s, with most of the University of Wittenberg moved to Jena because of the plague, he lectured on 1 John. His sermons on 1 and 2 Peter and Jude also became a standard evangelical commentary on those texts. Otherwise, apart from his lectures on Galatians from the 1530s, Luther interpreted Isaiah, the Minor Prophets, Deuteronomy, Psalms, and at the end of his career, Genesis.

of this slightly built man in August 1518 sent Luther over the moon, assured that the fledging university (founded in 1502) had found just the right scholar for the position. To his Erfurt friend and fellow Augustinian Johannes Lang, Luther had described a year earlier his excitement with the humanist turn ("our theology") Wittenberg's curriculum had taken.

> Our theology and St. Augustine are continuing to succeed and they reign in our university through God's action. Aristotle slowly is falling, headed for eternal ruin in the near future. Remarkably, lectures by the teachers of the *Sentences* are loathed. Nor can any-one hope to have anyone attending lectures unless they want to confess this theology, that is, the Bible, or St. Augustine or some other teacher of ecclesiastical authority.[7]

Melanchthon's knowledge of Greek and his sophisticated use of Latin were unique. While Erasmus had meticulously taught himself Greek as an adult, Melanchthon had already begun to learn the language in 1507 as an eleven-year-old student at the Latin school in Pforzheim. He also possessed a keen feel for all three "classical" languages (Latin, Greek, and Hebrew) and wrote grammars for Latin and Greek. It meant that he could sense, for example, when Paul was using Hebraisms in his language.[8] Whereas Erasmus judged Paul's Greek wanting compared to the classics by Homer, Demosthenes, or Plato, Melanchthon rejected such a prejudice and proclaimed Paul a far better stylist than Erasmus thought—coming to this conclusion even before the concept of Koine Greek (common Greek of the Greek and Roman Empires) had developed.

Translating the Bible

Wittenberg's translation of the Bible took a village. The role of Melanchthon in the production of Luther's translation of

7. Martin Luther, Letter to Johannes Lang, dated May 18, 1517, LW 48:42 (WA Br 1:99, 8–13). For a nuanced understanding of Luther's relation to Aristotle, see Theodor Dieter, *Der junge Luther und Aristoteles: Eine historisch-systematische Unter-suchung zum Verhältnis von Theologie und Philosophie* (Berlin: De Gruyter, 2001).

8. For one of the most important examples of Melanchthon's recognition of Hebraisms in Paul, see the appendix.

the New Testament, first published in September 1522 (and, hence, called the September Testament), is well known in general but hard to define in its particulars. We know that Luther brought his translation with him from the Wartburg in March 1522 and that Melanchthon played a crucial role in seeing it through the presses.[9] His knowledge of Greek was so far superior to Luther's, however, that it is simply impossible to imagine that Melanchthon did not provide direct input into polishing Luther's translation. The degree to which he also influenced the marginal glosses is harder to fix firmly. In one major instance, however, we can measure his impact on one of the many prefaces to individual biblical books, namely, Romans. This preface shows countless parallels to Melanchthon's own *Annotations on Romans*, which Luther insisted on publishing without the younger man's permission in November 1522.[10] The preface for the September Testament, quickly published separately and translated into Latin, was one of Luther's most influential works, so much so that the reading of an English translation at Aldersgate Chapel in the eighteenth century caused John Wesley's heart to be "strangely warmed."[11]

The translation of the Bible was a monumental task for Wittenberg's professors and printers, with a completed version first available in 1534 and including the Old Testament, New Testament, and Apocrypha. Although rightly associated with Luther's name, this was in fact a communal work, with Melanchthon, Aurogallus, Justus Jonas, Johannes Bugenhagen, and (later) Caspar Cruciger Sr. directly involved in the translation and subsequent revisions.[12] The team met on Fridays and used Georg Rörer as their amanuensis, so that some of the protocols of

9. See Timothy J. Wengert, "Martin Luther's *September Testament*: The Untold Story," *The Report: A Journal of German-American History* 47 (2017): 51–61.

10. Timothy J. Wengert et al., "Report of a Working Group at the 1997 Luther Congress," *Luther-Jahrbuch* 66 (1999): 298–301. For excerpts of this preface, see below, pp. 35–39.

11. John Wesley, journal entry for May 24, 1738, in *The Journal of John Wesley* ed. Percy Livingstone Parker (Chicago: Moody Press, 1951), online at the Christian Classics Ethereal Library, https://tinyurl.com/ybv6ocpk. I am grateful to Irving Sandberg for having provided this reference.

12. See the frontispiece of this book, a nineteenth-century depiction of Luther, Melanchthon, Bugenhagen, and Caspar Cruciger Sr. working on the translation of the Bible. For a description of this etching, see Gerhard Schwinge, *Melanchthon in der*

their discussions of revisions have survived.[13] A onetime Wittenberg student, Johannes Mathesius, whose sermons on Luther's
life became one of the first evangelical biographies of his hero,
described their meetings this way:

> When the Doctor [Luther] had in preparation studied the printed
> Bible and in addition had investigated the work of Jewish scholars
> and other experts in language—for example, one time he had a
> German butcher slaughter several sheep in order to learn the names
> of the various parts—he would come into the "consistory" with
> his old Latin Bible [the Vulgate] and the new German Bible. He
> also always had a Hebrew text at hand. Mr. Philip [Melanchthon]
> brought the Greek text [the Septuagint], Doctor [Caspar]
> Cruciger [Sr.] brought, alongside the Hebrew text, the
> Chaldean [Aramaic] Bible. The professors had their Rabbis with
> them [i.e., commentaries on the text by Jewish scholars]. Dr. Pom-
> mer [i.e., "the Pomeranian" Johannes Bugenhagen] also had a
> Latin text in front of him, which he had truly mastered. Each had
> previously prepared himself well for the text that was up for discus-
> sion and had studied the Greek, Latin and Jewish commentaries on
> the passage. Then the presider [Luther] would bring up a text for
> discussion and let the participants, one after the other, have their
> say concerning the characteristics of the language or the exposition
> of the ancient teachers. Wonderful and instructive speeches were
> made during this work.[14]

The daunting task of translating the Bible into German raised
the hackles of some of Wittenberg's opponents and forced
Luther to defend certain aspects of his translation in a separate
tract.[15] From it we learn several things about Luther's approach
to the biblical text. He began by appearing to dismiss his critics
with such arrogance, saying in effect, "This is my translation,

Druckgraphik: Eine Auswahl aus dem 17. bis 19. Jahrhundert (Ubstadt-Weiher: Verlag
Regionalkultur, 2000), 108–9.

13. WA Bi 3-4.

14. J. Mathesius, *Ausgewählte Werke*, vol. 3, *Luthers Leben in Predigten*, ed. Georg
Loesche (Prague: Calve, 1906), 315–16, cited according to the translation in Birgit
Stolt, "Luther's Translation of the Bible," *Lutheran Quarterly* 28 (2014): 373–400.

15. Martin Luther, *On Translating: An Open Letter* (153), LW 35:175–202 (WA
30/2:627–46). For the following paragraphs, see Birgit Stolt, *"Laßt uns fröhlich springen!": Gefühlswelt und Gefühlsnavigierung in Luthers Reformationsarbeit* (Berlin: Weidler, 2012), and Stolt, "Luther's Translation."

and if you do not like it, too bad." But this suggests a far more sophisticated hermeneutic of translation than some give him credit. His dismissive attitude mocked his opponents' dependence on papal authority and revealed their complete intransigence regarding matters of translating. (Indeed, not until the Vatican II decree *Dei Verbum* was the way definitively open to modern Catholic translations from the original languages.) Luther understood clearly that his enemies would not accept any of his arguments.

Luther then turned to his supporters and others whom he assumed were more open-minded. To them he described the process of translating, concentrating on two major objections: the insertion of the word "alone" into the text of Romans 3:28 about faith and his translation of the "Ave Maria" in Luke 1:28. His completely different attitude toward this second group of people reveals a crucial, communal aspect of Wittenberg's biblical interpretation. Luther was not interested in supporting "lone rangers" in biblical translation or interpretation. The conversation that took place in Wittenberg on Fridays mirrored his invitation to fellow believers to look over his shoulder and watch how he made decisions in translation (which were at the same time exegetical decisions).

But the conversation also involved the reader, whom Luther addressed directly in the introductions and glosses, material that was as important a part of his translation as the text itself. This passion for providing the Christian assembly and believers with an understandable text puts the lie to our age's more academic approach to Scripture. The Bible finds its home among believers in the church (where Lutherans define church as the assembling of believers around Word and Sacraments [that is, as the "event" of sharing the gospel]). While "neutral parties" and even "cultured despisers" may provide significant help understanding words and phrases, authorial intent, and historical context, the full meaning of the text will inevitably escape them—as indicated by their own neutrality or unbelief.

Before the term was invented, Luther was also a proponent of "dynamic equivalencies" in translation. That is, he understood that one could not simply import Hebraic or Greek syntax and grammar into German and assume such literal translation was legitimate. Here, too, the reader (a German-speaking believer) played a central role. On importing the word "alone" into the translation of Romans (making Paul say [in German] that we are justified "by faith alone"), Luther pointed out that German grammar demands the word, which Paul's Greek text clearly assumed. When the Greek (or Latin) author says, "Not X but Y," the implication must be made explicit in German: "not X but Y alone." As much as later scholars may wish that this decision represented a reading into the text of the Wittenbergers' own theological predilections, it is far more accurate to see this as derived from their very close reading of the biblical text in its original languages. As they experienced it, Paul's actual language and syntax forced them to confess and thus translate that the sinner is saved by faith alone.

In the 1530s, shortly after Luther published this tract, Melanchthon began to make the same argument in Latin but using the technical language of rhetoric. Romans, he argued, contains a series of "exclusive clauses" (*particulae exclusivae*), such as "not by works," "by faith," "apart from the law," and the like, all of which the Wittenbergers summarized with the phrase *sola fide* (by faith alone). This term was so important for later Lutherans that Martin Chemnitz introduced it into the text of the Formula of Concord.[16] In any event, both Luther with his defense of his translation of Paul and Melanchthon with his summary of Paul's syntax were insisting on reading Paul strictly within his own grammatical context but in a dynamic enough way to make allowances for differences between Greek and German.

The "Hail, Mary" posed another problem for Luther. In German the phrase "full of" (as in "Hail, Mary, full of grace") presented a linguistic impossibility for Luther, who pointed out that in German usage only concrete objects can be filled with things (such as a purse full of gold). Mary could hardly be (literally) "filled up" with some material substance called "grace." To solve this problem, Luther did two things simultaneously, only one of which has captured the attention of later scholars. In the first instance, given the impossibility of a literal translation (based on

---

16. *Formula of Concord*, Solid Declaration, 3.36, in BC 568.

the standard Latin), Luther made his famous plea to *schau das Volk aufs Maul* (look the people in the mouth).[17] Indeed, we know from Mathesius and others just how far Luther went to see to it that his translation matched the common German terms for certain things. Based on this plea, later translators argued that Luther simply used common, vulgar language in his translation.

As Birgit Stolt has proved, however, Luther was also sensitive to the odd Hebraic nature of the New Testament. Thus he argued in this tract that to understand the angel's greeting, one has to see how Gabriel greeted people in the Old Testament (especially in Daniel) and to realize that the New Testament greeting corresponded to the Hebrew. In this way, rather than simply adhering to a single rule of using everyday German, Luther also respected the oddities of the Greek and Hebrew and imported them into the text, so as to startle the reader into realizing that the text was not his or her own but remained somehow foreign—in this case filled with divine meaning. Thus, even though Luther knew that "Hail, Mary, full of grace" could be translated, "Dear Mary" (or, as one English translation later put it, "Hello, Mary"), he refrained from doing so and instead preserved the angel's unique, Hebraic way of speaking. This mixture of dynamic equivalence and attention to Hebraisms resulted in a far more sophisticated translation than many have realized. For example, Luther started many sentences in the Old Testament with the un-German "and" (preserving the original *waw* [and] from the Hebrew). Like Luke (who was indeed imitating Hebraic style), Luther included phrases like "Behold" (for *hinneh*) and "It came to pass" (for *egeneto*). Luther's practice was so influential that the King James Bible, following its predecessors, continued to do much the same thing. Thus we find in Luther's translation both a desire that the authors speak German and an insistence on letting the same authors' linguistic idiosyncrasies come to expression. In sum, Luther's translation was at the same time inviting and alienating, a remarkable accomplishment and a crucial aspect of his hermeneutics.

---

17. As Stolt points out, *Maul* in the sixteenth century was simply the standard word for mouth and only later became associated with animals and thus seems derogatory to modern ears. See Stolt, "Luther's Translation," 399n12.

The struggle over the Ave Maria, however, also arose out of a dramatic shift in how the Wittenberg theologians understood the Greek word *charis* (χάρις, usually translated *gratia* [grace] in the Latin).[18] In his 1516 *Annotations* on the New Testament, Erasmus had pointed out that the word *charis* did not mean what scholastic theologians had said *gratia* meant. They insisted that *gratia* was a habit or disposition of love (*caritas*) infused into the soul through the sacraments of baptism and penance, moving that soul from a state of sin into a state of grace. Thus this form of grace was defined as the *gratia gratum faciens*, the grace that makes (the soul) acceptable (to God). Given this ontological reading, it would then not be impossible for someone (in terms of their essence at least) to be filled with grace. Erasmus, on the contrary, insisted that in the Greek the word simply meant God's favor (*favor Dei*). In 1519, when Luther published his first commentary on Galatians, he was not fully convinced by Erasmus's arguments and opted for a both/and solution: in Paul the word *charis* means both "God's favor" *and* "an infused disposition." By 1520, however, Philip Melanchthon seems to have taken up Erasmus's arguments, and in 1521, in an attack on the Louvain theologian Latomus, Luther too had changed his mind and made fun of Latomus for insisting on an ontological definition of grace as some sort of quality or disposition infused into the soul rather than as God's favor and mercy. This, too, made it impossible for Luther to translate the Lucan text as "full of grace" (as if grace were a substance poured into Mary's soul). Instead, he insisted on a very different approach, rendering the angel's greeting as *Holdselige Maria* (gracious, favored Mary).

As Christians today assemble around Word and Sacrament, often the first thing to go is the actual words of the biblical text. At best, they are jumping-off points for a preacher's own moralistic speculation: "Given that the angel calls Mary gracious, how might we today do the same thing for our neighbor?" This may not be a bad admonition, but it leaves the scandal of a

---

18. Rolf Schäfer, "Melanchthon's Interpretation of Romans 5:15: His Departure from the Augustinian Concept of Grace Compared to Luther's," in *Philip Melanchthon (1497–1560) and the Commentary*, ed. Timothy J. Wengert and M. Patrick Graham (Sheffield: Sheffield Academic, 1997), 79–104.

young woman bearing the "Son of the Almighty" in the dust. Or, again, the word *faith* in Romans becomes "the faith of Jesus" (a literal and inept rendering of the Greek [and Latin!] genitive), so that justification by faith actually means imitating Jesus by producing a faith similar to his. "Come on, little ones, you, too, can believe just as Jesus did!" Then the "by grace you are saved through faith" of Ephesians 2 becomes submerged in the work of faith that hearers must accomplish (or else!). Then, too, the complex nature of the genitive case—which one could render much more successfully as either a subjective or an objective genitive, that is, as either the faith (= trust) that Jesus creates in us (Rom 10:17: "faith comes by hearing . . .") or the faith that trusts Jesus—disappears.[19] The Wittenbergers force us back to the actual text of Scripture, to wring from it what it is defining for us and doing to us.

The Authors of Scripture

In the ancient and medieval church, exegetes did not ignore the fact that there were human authors behind the texts they were interpreting. This perspective was especially true for the apostle Paul, who served as a model for Christian interpreters of the Bible.[20] In the Middle Ages, exegetes like Thomas Aquinas or Nicholas of Lyra clearly assumed that David and others wrote the psalms in very particular contexts and that by employing certain aspects of dialectics (especially the *divisio* [dividing the text according to things like causes, form and matter, and other Aristotelian categories]) they could get close to the human author's own mind, who (they were convinced) had undoubtedly operated with such categories in their writings.

The Renaissance, however, rediscovered authors as intention-

---

19. As is so often the case with our age's "new perspectives" on Paul, the fact that the Vulgate's literal rendering (as a genitive) gave no interpreter grounds to imagine that the "faith of Jesus" meant anything other than "faith in Jesus" throughout the entire history of exegesis of Romans has had no impact on their arbitrary (and law-centered) rendering of the Greek genitive. See Erik Heen, "A Lutheran Response to the New Perspective on Paul," *Lutheran Quarterly* 24 (2010): 263–91.

20. Luigi Franco Pizzolato, *La dottrina esegetica di sant Ambrogio* (Milan: Vita e Pensiero, 1978).

ally employing rhetorical schemes and logical arguments to create whole literary works and convey meaning. This meant that for the first time ancient, authoritative authors (either the church fathers or the scriptural authors) could be viewed in toto and not simply as providers of pithy prooftexts for scholastic theological edifices to be excerpted in various catenae and quoted in theological summae. As heir to this Renaissance approach, Luther could describe his breakthrough on the doctrine of justification in 1545 as connected to reading a specific (entire!) text of Augustine (*On the Spirit and the Letter*). Thirty years earlier, Luther's lectures on Romans demonstrated the same approach to that tract (which was basically Augustine's interpretation of Romans), as Leif Grane demonstrated.[21] Similarly, Luther and his Wittenberg colleagues were also reading the biblical texts as if written by real authors using standard rhetorical techniques and making actual arguments.

We have no better example of this approach than Philip Melanchthon's lectures on Romans from 1520 to 1521, published at Luther's insistence in November 1522. For the first time ever, a Christian exegete tried to determine the contours of Paul's own arguments using Ciceronian rules of rhetoric.[22] This was so important for Melanchthon that at the end of the decade (in 1529–1530) he produced a separate commentary devoted exclusively to determining the rhetorical (and, for one major section, dialectical) structure of Romans.[23] Two years later, in 1532, he then used that information to help shape his *Commentaries on Romans*, a much more expansive exegetical work.[24] His method was so influential that his student and fellow lecturer on the Pauline corpus, Georg Major, produced a similar outline for every Pauline epistle.[25]

21. Leif Grane, *Modus loquendi theologicus: Luthers Kampf um die Erneuerung der Theologie (1515–1518)* (Leiden: Brill, 1975).

22. Timothy J. Wengert, "Philip Melanchthon's 1522 Annotations on Romans and the Lutheran Origins of Rhetorical Criticism," in *Biblical Interpretation in the Era of the Reformation*, ed. Richard A. Muller and John L. Thompson (Grand Rapids: Eerdmans, 1996), 118–40.

23. CR 15:443–92.

24. The editor of the 1532 *Commentaries*, Rolf Schäfer, provides a handy outline of Melanchthon's approach in MSA 5:373–78.

25. See Timothy J. Wengert, "Georg Major (1502–1574): Defender of the Wit-

The impact on Wittenberg's exegesis was profound. For the first time ever exegetes were analyzing specific literary arguments of a biblical author. To a lesser extent, Melanchthon even used this method to analyze specific sermons (Latin: *conciones*, i.e., "speeches") of Jesus, especially in the Gospel of John.[26] Indeed, Melanchthon's reputation in this regard continued into twentieth-century interpretation, which revived "rhetorical criticism" as a discipline and never failed to pay its respects to Melanchthon's original innovation. What this and other literary approaches to biblical texts succeeded in doing was to bring the human author into far clearer focus. Scripture was no longer simply a trove of doctrinal or moral principles, loosely strung on beads by biblical authors at the dictation of the Holy Spirit. Instead, the authors themselves were understood as having a voice and employing logical arguments and rhetorical turns of phrase to make their cases. Moreover, their ways of presenting the bases for their claims were available to later readers, who could use all of the rhetorical and dialectical tools at their disposal to unlock the meaning of a text by asking not simply, What is this author saying? but also, Why is he saying it in this way?

This level of sophistication was absent from many of Melanchthon's contemporaries, including Erasmus, who belittled Paul's abilities with Greek and in one of his prefaces to the New Testament suggested that readers sort texts according to standard categories (Latin: *nidulae* [nestlets]) of moral philosophy.[27] This approach made the first-century author's own concerns far less important to later exegetes, so much so that Erasmus dismissed the first eleven chapters of Romans as merely dealing with a problem in Jewish law (circumcision) and urged the reader to concentrate instead on the moral exhortations of chapters 12–15. This is why Luther and Melanchthon's preface to Romans for the September Testament represented such

tenberg's Faith and Melanchthonian Exegete," in *Melanchthon in seinen Schülern*, ed. Heinz Scheible (Wiesbaden: Harrassowitz, 1997), 129–56.

26. See Timothy J. Wengert, *Philip Melanchthon's "Annotationes in Johannem" of 1523 in Relation to Its Predecessors and Contemporaries* (Geneva: Droz, 1987).

27. Timothy J. Wengert, *Human Freedom, Christian Righteousness: Philip Melanchthon's Exegetical Dispute with Erasmus of Rotterdam* (New York: Oxford University Press, 1998), 56–64.

an innovation (and a not-so-subtle attack on Erasmus, without naming names). Paul's use of important terms ("law," "gospel," "justification," "grace," "faith," etc.) and the sweep of his argument in Romans 1–11 mattered! These arguments spoke not only to Paul's own audience but also, by virtue of the epistle's clear structure, to later Christians as well.

The *Argumentum*: Searching for the Heart of Each Biblical Book and Chapter

Once an interpreter begins to focus on the biblical author's contribution to Scripture, a second question arises: What is the author's point? In other words, how best does one summarize a particular book of the Bible? This aspect of biblical interpretation, labeled in sixteenth-century commentaries the *argumentum* (basic argument), always played some role in ancient and medieval Christian exegesis. The Vulgate itself came with prefaces, attributed to Jerome, that briefly summarized each book of the Bible. In the Middle Ages, commentators like Nicholas of Lyra began their commentaries with analyses of those prefaces and then provided detailed outlines dividing the book into its logical components. But it was Renaissance authors, especially Erasmus of Rotterdam, who provided new and expanded introductions to the New Testament books, ones that commented not only on the Latin text but also on the Greek original. It is from the preface to Romans, for example, that we learn of Erasmus's low opinion of Paul's Greek style and his dismissal of the first eleven chapters as dealing with only a completely irrelevant issue (the role of Jewish ceremonial law in the Christian faith).

Luther and especially Melanchthon took this interest in a biblical book's point to a whole new level. For one thing, they ignored for the most part the prefaces of Jerome and pseudo-Jerome (actually Pelagius), as well as those of earlier exegetes, and wrote their own, sometimes taking issue (again, without naming names) with Erasmus's work. For another, especially Melanchthon assumed that making a rhetorical outline of a work contributed to understanding what the author was trying to accomplish. This single-minded interest in the central point of a biblical book or even individual chapters led Melanchthon to write commentaries that skipped passages. He assumed that if the readers knew the central point of a particular chapter, they could easily interpret the remaining verses on their own, because he expected commentaries to function as outlines or scaffolding that could draw the readers into the text and not stand in their way. John Calvin, whose introduction to humanist exegesis came through Andrea Alciato, the Renaissance professor of law in Bourges, criticized Melanchthon's Roman commentary on this very basis.[28] To be sure, Luther also went verse by verse through texts, but his method arose more out of his own meditative, quasi-monastic way of reading the Bible. As a result, his commentaries contained lengthy meditations on single verses that ranged freely from the biblical author's context to Luther's.[29] Moreover, in his commentaries and sermons he still managed to keep the author's main argument squarely in view.

In 1522, Melanchthon had just completed lectures on Romans, and Luther, with Melanchthon's help, was writing the lengthy preface to Romans for the September Testament. Both agreed that Romans held a special place in the Bible. Some have accused them of establishing a "canon within the canon," using their own idiosyncratic theologies to overemphasize justification by faith alone. This ignores the principle, gleaned from the humanists of their day, that every book had a central point revealed by the author. Insofar as God was the author of Scripture, Luther and Melanchthon were convinced that Romans provided that very center for Scripture. This did not mean that they sought to twist every other book to match Paul's message. Indeed, even within the Pauline corpus they recognized differences, as did their students. Instead, Romans gave the reader of Scripture the best lens through which to evaluate the biblical texts. Otherwise, human reason and its addiction

28. Wengert, *Melanchthon's "Annotationes in Johannem,"* 183, referring to CO 38:404. As a lawyer, Calvin realized that to make a theological argument the exegete had to take into account all of the facts of a text. Thus, although, like Melanchthon, he read the text with a humanist's eyes, he could sometimes obscure the underlying thrust of a biblical author's arguments.

29. See esp. Kenneth Hagen, *Luther's Approach to Scripture as Seen in His "Commentaries" on Galatians 1519–1538* (Tübingen: Mohr Siebeck, 1993).

to works would inevitably skew the meaning of Scripture and obscure the divine and human authorial intent.

This was by no means the only center that Martin Luther discovered in Scripture. In the *Large Catechism* (and mirrored in the *Small Catechism*) Luther insisted that the first commandment ("You shall have no other gods before me," Exod 20:3; Deut 5:7) was the center of the Ten Commandments, the psalms, and, finally, all Scripture.[30] Elsewhere, he could call John 3:16 "the gospel in a nutshell." With Melanchthon as Wittenberg's chief New Testament exegete giving regular lectures on Romans, Luther turned to other books, especially Galatians, Psalms, and (for the last ten years of his life) Genesis.

Melanchthon, too, interpreted many other books of the Bible.[31] His *loci* method for doing theology actually broadened his understanding of Romans as, to use his words, the *doctrinae Christianae compendium* (summary of Christian teaching).[32] Romans did not have exclusive access to the gospel but rather shared (perhaps more fully than other books) in this overarching topic of "gospel." Thus other books, chapters, or verses also could express the *summa Evangelii* (summation of the gospel). Whatever help Romans gave in interpreting Scripture, it was hardly alone, and it gained its authority from its participation in the underlying message of the gospel and the gospel's singular effect on hearers.

One splendid example from Luther about how the *argumentum* functioned may be seen in his brief commentary on Psalms from 1531 to 1533. Not only did he list at the outset the twenty-one different themes found in the psalms, but he also used the preface to announce that he had finished revisions of his translation of Psalms (for the entire Bible, published in 1534) around Easter 1531 and therefore felt he needed to provide an overview of the psalms (which he finally completed in late 1533). The preface also included a defense of individual decisions about translation throughout the Psalter. Then it set out

30. Martin Luther, LC (1529), Ten Commandments, par. 324–29, in BC 429–30.
31. Timothy J. Wengert, "The Biblical Commentaries of Philip Melanchthon," in Wengert and Graham, *Philip Melanchthon*, 106–48.
32. Philip Melanchthon, *Commonplaces: Loci Communes 1521*, trans. Christian Preus (St. Louis: Concordia, 2014), 25 (= MSA 2/1:21).

Luther's analysis of its five genres. First, some psalms contained prophecies either of Christ, of the church, or of the saints. This genre included all psalms "that contain pledges and love, promises to the righteous and threats to the godless."[33] The other four genres were instructional psalms (that condemned human doctrine and praised God's word), psalms of comfort for the sorrowing saints (and terror for tyrants), prayers of the faithful in all kinds of need (including laments), and psalms of thanksgiving. But Luther admitted that some psalms combine several or even all of these aspects in one. Nevertheless, in his summaries, Luther tended to announce at the very beginning the particular theme (he often used the Latin *scopus*—a favorite of Melanchthon as well—to describe what he found). Thus, for example, Psalm 1 is a psalm of comfort; Psalm 2 is a prophecy of Christ; Psalm 3 is a prayer; and Psalm 4 is again a psalm of comfort. Laments are often introduced with "this is a prayer psalm and lament."[34]

Perhaps Luther's most famous *Argumentum* is what he prepared as an introduction to his 1522 translation of Romans. Written in collaboration with Melanchthon, Luther's preface would continue to be printed with his translation into the nineteenth century. It represents a perfect blending of Renaissance exegetical concerns with Wittenberg's hermeneutic.

> This Epistle is really the chief part of the New Testament, and is truly the purest gospel. It is worthy not only that each and every Christian should know it word for word, by heart, but also that they should occupy themselves with it every day, as the daily bread of the soul. We can never read it or ponder over it too much; for the more we deal with it, the more precious it becomes and the better it tastes.
>
> Therefore I, too, will do my best, so far as God has given me power, to open the way into it through this preface, so that it may be the better understood by everyone. Heretofore it has been badly

33. WA 38:17: "Und hie herein gehören alle Psalmen, da Promissiones et mine, verheissungen den frumen und drewung uber die Gottlosen innen sind." I am reading "mine" as "minne."

34. For example, WA 38:21 on Psalm 12. For specific psalms, see chap. 5, pp. 135–56. These summaries were so popular that Veit Dietrich, a student of Luther and Melanchthon and pastor in Nuremberg, included them in his own summary of the Bible, giving credit to them for his own summaries. See Veit Dietrich, *Summaria uber die gantze Bibel* (Nuremberg: Vom Berg & Newber, 1545).

obscured by glosses and all kinds of idle talk, though in itself it is a bright light, almost sufficient to illuminate the entire Holy Scriptures.

To begin with, we must have knowledge of its language and know what St. Paul means by the words "law," "sin," "grace," "faith," "righteousness," "flesh," "spirit," and the like. Otherwise no reading of the book has any value.[35]

After defining the word "law," Luther concludes,

So it happens that faith alone makes a person righteous and fulfills the law. For out of the merit of Christ it brings forth the Spirit. And the Spirit makes the heart glad and free, as the law requires that it shall be. Thus, good works emerge from faith itself. That is what St. Paul means in chapter 3[:31]; after he has rejected the works of the law, it sounds as if he would overthrow the law by this faith. "No," he says, "we uphold the law by faith"; that is, we fulfill it by faith.[36]

In his discussion of sin, Luther remarks,

Hence, Christ calls unbelief the only sin, when he says in John 16[:8–9], "The Spirit will convince the world of sin . . . because they do not believe in me." For this reason, too, before good or bad works take place, as the good or bad fruits, there must first be in the heart faith or unbelief. Unbelief is the root, the sap, and the chief power of all sin. . . .[37]

Between grace and gift there is this difference. Grace actually means God's favor, or the good will which in himself he bears toward us, by which he is disposed to give us Christ and to pour into us the Holy Spirit with his gifts. This is clear from chapter 5[:15], where St. Paul speaks of "the grace and gift in Christ," etc. The gifts and the Spirit increase in us every day, but they are not yet perfect since there remain in us the evil desires and sins that war against the Spirit, as he says in Rom. 7[:5ff.] and Gal. 5[:17]. . . . Nevertheless, grace does so much that we are accounted completely righteous before God. For his grace is not divided or parceled out, as are the gifts, but takes us completely into favor for the sake of Christ our Intercessor and Mediator. And because of this, the gifts are begun in us.

35. AL 6:464.
36. AL 6:466.
37. AL 6:467.

In this sense, then, you can understand chapter 7. There St. Paul still calls himself a sinner; and yet he can say, in chapter 8[:1], that there is no condemnation for those who are in Christ simply because of the incompleteness of the gifts and of the Spirit. Because the flesh is not yet slain, we are still sinners. But because we believe in Christ and have a beginning of the Spirit, God is so favorable and gracious to us that he will not count the sin against us or judge us because of it. Rather, he deals with us according to our faith in Christ, until sin is slain.

Faith is not the human notion and dream that some people call faith. When they see that no improvement of life and no good works follow—although they can hear and say much about faith—they fall into the error of saying, "Faith is not enough; one must do works in order to be righteous and be saved." This is due to the fact that when they hear the gospel, they get busy and by their own powers create an idea in their heart which says, "I believe"; they take this then to be true faith. But, as it is a human figment and idea that never reaches the depths of the heart, nothing comes of it either, and no improvement follows.

Faith, however, is a divine work in us which changes us and makes us to be born anew of God, John 1[:12–13]. It kills the old Adam and makes us altogether different, in heart and spirit and mind and powers; and it brings with it the Holy Spirit. O, it is a living, busy, active, mighty thing, this faith. It is impossible for it not to be doing good works incessantly. It does not ask whether good works are to be done, but before the question is asked, it has already done them, and is constantly doing them. Whoever does not do such works, however, is an unbeliever. A person gropes and looks around for faith and good works, but knows neither what faith is nor what good works are. Yet that one talks and talks, with many words, about faith and good works.

Faith is a living, daring confidence in God's grace, so sure and certain that the believer would stake his [or her] life on it a thousand times.[38] This knowledge of and confidence in God's grace makes people glad and bold and happy in dealing with God and with all creatures. And this is the work which the Holy Spirit performs in faith. Because of it, without compulsion, a person is ready and glad to do good to everyone, to serve everyone, to suffer everything, out of love and praise to God who has shown this grace. Thus, it is impossible to separate works from faith, quite as

38. This phrase and others like it are sometimes quoted out of context (where Luther clearly states that faith is God's work in the human being) and thus used to turn faith into a decision of the will and work.

impossible as to separate heat and light from fire. Beware, therefore, of your own false notions and of the idle talkers who imagine
themselves wise enough to make decisions about faith and good
works, and yet are the greatest fools. Pray God that he may work
faith in you. Otherwise you will surely remain forever without
faith, regardless of what you may think or do.

Righteousness, then, is such a faith. It is called "the righteousness
of God" because God gives it, and counts it as righteousness for
the sake of Christ our Mediator, and makes us to fulfill our oblig-
ations to everybody. For through faith we become free from sin
and come to take pleasure in God's commandments, thereby we
give God the honor due him, and pay him what we owe him.[39]
Likewise, we serve others willingly, by whatever means we can,
and thus pay our debts to everyone. Nature, free will, and our own
powers cannot bring this righteousness into being. For as no one
can give himself [or herself] faith, neither can he [or she] take away
his [or her] own unbelief. . . .[40]

Flesh and spirit you must not understand as though flesh is
only that which has to do with unchastity and spirit is only that
which has to do with what is inwardly in the heart. Rather, like
Christ in John 3[:6], Paul calls everything "flesh" that is born
of the flesh—the whole person, with body and soul, mind and
senses—because everything about us longs for the flesh. Thus, you
should learn to call one "fleshly," too, who thinks, teaches, and talks
a great deal about lofty spiritual matters, yet does so without grace.
. . .[41]

On the contrary, you should call a person "spiritual" who is
occupied with the most external kind of works, as Christ was when
he washed the disciples' feet [John 13:1–14], and Peter when he
steered his boat and fished. Thus, "the flesh" is a person who lives
and works, inwardly and outwardly, in the service of the flesh's
gain and of this temporal life. "The spirit" is the one who loves and
works, inwardly and outwardly, in the service of the Spirit and of
the future life.

Without such a grasp of [all] these words, you will never understand this letter of St. Paul, nor any other book of Holy Scripture.
Therefore beware of all teachers who use these words in a different

39. Here Luther is using the customary (Ciceronian) definition of righteousness
as "to each his [or her] own," except that here, as in the *Freedom of a Christian*, he
describes the sinner giving God his due.
40. AL 6:468–70.
41. Al 6:470.

sense, no matter who they are, even Origen, Ambrose,[42] Augustine, Jerome, and others like them or even above them. . . .[43]

After an extensive description of each chapter, Luther concludes,

> In this epistle we thus find most abundantly the things that a Chris-
> tian ought to know, namely, what is law, gospel, sin, punishment,
> grace, faith, righteousness, Christ, God, good works, love, hope,
> and the cross; and also how we are to conduct ourselves toward
> everyone, [whether] righteous or sinner, strong or weak, friend or
> foe—and even toward our own selves. Moreover, this is all ably
> supported with Scripture and proved by St. Paul's own example
> and that of the prophets, so that one could not wish for anything
> more. Therefore it appears that he wanted in this one epistle to
> sum up briefly the whole Christian and evangelical doctrine, and
> to prepare an introduction to the entire Old Testament. For with-
> out doubt, [all] who [have] this epistle well in [their] heart have
> with [them] the light and power of the Old Testament. Therefore
> let all Christians be familiar with it and exercise themselves in it
> continually. To this end may God give his grace. Amen.[44]

Loci Communes (Central Topics) and the Unity of Scripture

Wittenberg's preface to Romans reveals another aspect of their
exegetical method: the *locus communis* (plural: *loci communes*). In
Renaissance thought north of the Alps there were two compet-
ing approaches to finding the central themes and topics of biblical texts. On the one side, as mentioned above, Erasmus of
Rotterdam in one of his prefaces to his edition of the Greek New
Testament urged readers to develop what he termed "nestlets"
(*nidulae*), cubbyholes into which one could sort the diverse topics found in the Bible. His lengthy list included for the most part
themes closely related to his own interests in moral philosophy.
On the other side, Rudolf Agricola developed an understanding of *loci communes* that were more germane to the text being
analyzed and developed out of a careful use of not only rhetoric

---

42. Luther probably means "Ambrosiaster" (pseudo-Ambrose), a fifth-century
Latin theologian who wrote a commentary on the entire Pauline corpus.
43. AL 6:470–71.
44. AL 6:479.

(as with Erasmus) but also logic (dialectics). Melanchthon, to whom his fellow student at the University of Tübingen, Johann Oecolampadius (later Reformer in Basel), had given a copy of Agricola's work, then turned this tool toward the interpretation of the Bible. He rejected Erasmus's approach as disturbing the author's own intentions by imposing a host of (classical) moral topics onto Scripture. Instead, using especially (but not exclusively) Romans, Melanchthon developed a series of topics that arose directly out of Paul's own writing: free will, sin, law, gospel, grace, faith, righteousness, and the like. In 1521 (at the ripe old age of twenty-four), he published his results in a book he titled *Loci communes rerum theologicarum seu hypotyposes theologicae* (Wittenberg: Melchior Lotter, 1521), or *Commonplaces of Theological Matters or Theological Outlines* (the word *hypotyposes* is borrowed from the Greek).[45] By using Romans as his guide, Melanchthon sought to overcome what he saw as a weakness in his medieval predecessors, who in his opinion (like Erasmus) used topics and organizational schemes foreign to Scripture to organize their theological systems.

This approach to Scripture helped to identify the central themes of radically different books. Thus it served to unify Scripture in a way quite different from what exegetes had used in the past, arguing that all (or almost all) of the biblical authors were concerned with matters of faith, sin and grace, life and death, and that by drawing together what they said the theologian gained a far deeper view of what these authors were thinking. The problem with such an approach, however, is that, when used outside of the previous insistence on identifying the author's own basic argument, texts could be ripped from their context and made to serve external, extrabiblical ends. Then the author's own words become subsumed into a greater effort to

45. The second Latin edition came out in 1536, titled *Loci communes theologici recens collecti et recogniti* [Theological *loci communes* recently drawn together and revised] (Wittenberg: Klug, 1536). It was followed in 1543 with the *Loci communes theologici recens recogniti* [Theological *loci communes* recently revised] (Wittenberg: Seitz, 1543). The German version of the second edition, translated by Justus Jonas and published in 1536, and revised by Melanchthon himself for publication in 1555, was titled *Die Hauptartikel Christlicher Lehre . . . im latin genant Loci communes Theologici* [The chief articles of Christian teaching . . . called in Latin *loci communes*] (Wittenberg, 1536 and 1555).

discover an ideational unity that might have had little or nothing to do with the author's own intent. Yet without some method of unifying the biblical message, the texts could easily fly apart and the interpreter be left with no way to discover the Bible's theological center.

NOT JUST FACTS BUT EFFECT

A Renaissance Debate

As we have seen, one hot topic for debate during the Renaissance was the relation between rhetoric (oratory) and dialectics (logic). Scholastic theologians had almost unanimously supported the priority of dialectics—a decision for which their humanist detractors mocked them. Thinkers like Erasmus championed the hegemony of rhetoric, since it was geared to move hearts rather than convince the intellect. Other thinkers, especially Rudolf Agricola, sought instead to blend the two: insisting that, for example, the judicial genre of speech required a section (the so-called *confirmatio*) that proved the speaker's point and had to rest not simply on emotional arguments but solid, logical proof. Certainty arose only by using certain and sure forms of arguments and proofs, not by merely appealing to the will. Once Oecolampadius gave Melanchthon a copy of Rudolf Agricola's work on logic, Melanchthon insisted on combining dialectics and rhetoric in writing and thinking. By 1521, in his second handbook on rhetoric (the *Institutiones rhetoricae*), Melanchthon had even expanded the number of speech genres from Cicero's and Quintilian's three (judicial, demonstrative, and deliberative) to four, adding classroom lecture, which used dialectics for its rules of invention. As Melanchthon never tired of repeating, rhetoric dealt in probabilities and dialectics in certainties. Both were necessary, but each in its proper place.

For Melanchthon, dialectics (as he stated already in his first handbook on the subject, from 1520) involved not only the use of logical syllogisms but also the ten questions of Aristotle's *Analytics*, which included: whether a thing existed, what a thing was, what were its parts, its genus and species, and its causes. But Melanchthon, in both his exegesis and his theological writings, favored two questions: what a thing is (*Quid sit*, a category closely related to logic) and what its effects were (*Quid effectus*, a category at home in rhetoric).[46] This insistence led Melanchthon in his first edition of the *Loci communes*, from 1521, to ask two questions of many topics, including: "What Is Sin?" and "What Is the Power of Sin?"; "What Is Law?" and "What Is the Power of Law?"; and "What Is Gospel?" and "What Is the Power of the Gospel?" The move from definition of a thing to its effects is scattered throughout Melanchthon's exegetical works as well. Indeed, for both Luther and Melanchthon the meaning of a particular doctrine always involved both questions, so that defining "right doctrine" was never the only demand placed on theologians. They also needed to ask what a particular interpretation of a text or doctrine did to its hearers. Despite Sergeant Friday's plea, to do theology properly, "the facts" were never enough and, taken alone, often distorted the very teaching that the theologian was struggling to defend.

We find Luther using the same categories in his catechisms of 1529, where especially on the sacraments he first provides a definition (e.g., "What Is Baptism?") but then immediately describes the benefits or effects (e.g., "What Are Baptism's Benefits?"). Already seven years earlier, when Luther left the protective custody of the Wartburg to return to his pulpit at St. Mary's, Wittenberg's city church, he underscored the difference between

---

46. This latter question is actually the fourth of Aristotle's four causes (efficient, material, formal, and final), where the final cause has to do with the goal of a thing and, hence, its effect or power. See Wengert, *Melanchthon's "Annotationes in Johannem,"* 167–212. One question (whether a thing exists), completely disregarded by Melanchthon, was very important for other thinkers of the age, including Ulrich Zwingli, who began his *Commentary on True and False Religion* by asking whether religion existed. Luther and Melanchthon viewed such questions in theology to be highly speculative and thus dangerous. In the 1550s, Andreas Osiander dabbled in similar speculation when he asked whether Christ would have come had Adam and Eve not sinned. By and large his critics—with the exception of John Calvin—ignored this (by Wittenberg's standards) frivolous question and focused on Osiander's attack on justification by faith. See Timothy J. Wengert, "Philip Melanchthon and John Calvin against Andreas Osiander: Coming to Terms with Forensic Justification," in *Calvin and Luther: The Continuing Relationship*, ed. R. Ward Holder (Göttingen: Vandenhoeck & Ruprecht, 2013), 63–87.

merely holding right doctrine and the true goal of Christian teaching: love and patience for the weak. In his dramatic first sermon, delivered on the first Sunday in Lent 1522 (designated in the sixteenth century as "Invocavit Sunday," from which these eight sermons get their name), he said,

> The summons of death comes to us all, and no one can die for another. Every one must fight his [or her] own battle with death by himself [or herself] alone. We can shout into another's ears, but every one must himself [or herself] be prepared for the time of death, for I will not be with you then, nor you with me. Therefore every one must know and be armed [in the heart] with the chief things which concern a Christian. And these are what you, my beloved, have heard from me many days ago.
>
> In the first place, we must know that we are the children of wrath, and all our works, intentions, and thoughts are nothing at all. Here we need a clear, strong text to bear out this point. Such is the saying of St. Paul in Eph. 2[:3]. Note this well; and though there are many such in the Bible, I do not wish to overwhelm you with many texts. "We are children of wrath." And please do not undertake to say: I have built an altar, given a foundation for masses, etc.
>
> Secondly, that God has sent us his only-begotten Son, that we may believe in him and that whoever trust in him shall be free from sin and a child of God, as John declares in his first chapter, "To all who believed in his name, he gave power to become children of God" [John 1:12]. Here we should all be well versed in the Bible and ready to confront the devil with many passages. With respect to these two points I do not feel that there has been anything wrong or lacking. They have been rightly preached to you, and I should be sorry if it were otherwise. Indeed, I am well aware and I dare say that you are more learned than I, and that there are not only one, two, three, or four, but perhaps ten or more, who have this knowledge and enlightenment.
>
> Thirdly, we must also have love and through love we must do to one another as God has done to us through faith. For without love faith is nothing, as St. Paul says (1 Cor. 2 [=13:1]): "If I had the tongues of angels and could speak of the highest things in faith, and have not love, I am nothing." And here, dear friends, have you not grievously failed? I see no signs of love among you, and I observe very well that you have not been grateful to God for his rich gifts and treasures.

Here let us beware lest Wittenberg become Capernaum [cf. Matt 11:23]. I notice that you have a great deal to say of the doctrine of faith and love which is preached to you, and this is no wonder; a donkey can almost intone the lessons, and why should you not be able to repeat the doctrines and formulas? Dear friends, the kingdom of God—and we are that kingdom—does not consist in talk or words [1 Cor 4:20], but in activity, in deeds, in works and exercises. God does not want hearers and repeaters of words [James 1:22], but followers and doers, and this occurs in faith through love. For a faith without love is not enough—rather it is not faith at all, but a counterfeit of faith, just as a face seen in a mirror is not a real face, but merely the reflection of a face [1 Cor 13:12].

Fourthly, we also need patience. For whoever has faith, trusts in God, and shows love to his neighbor, practicing it day by day, must needs suffer persecution. For the devil never sleeps, but constantly gives [such a one] plenty of trouble. But patience works and produces hope [Rom 5:4], which freely yields itself to God and vanishes away in him. Thus faith, by much affliction and persecution, ever increases, and is strengthened day by day. A heart thus blessed with virtues can never rest or restrain itself, but rather pours itself out again for the benefit and service of the brethren [and sisters], just as God has done to it.

And here, dear friends, one must not insist upon one's rights, but must see what may be useful and helpful to one's brother [or sister], as Paul says . . . "'All things are lawful for me,' but not all things are helpful" [1 Cor 6:12].[47]

This way of defining truth (as involving both definition and effect) remains foreign to many biblical interpreters today, where modern concerns for "facts" have drowned out the effect a text has on us.[48] Yet Wittenberg's exegetical method cannot be understood outside of the marriage of these two. For example, many scholars have noted that John Calvin's approach to the bondage of the will seems far closer to Luther's (in his tract from 1525, *On the Bondage of the Will*) than does Melanchthon's later approach.[49] Yet we know that in the 1530s, when for the

---

47. Martin Luther, *Invocavit Sermons* (1522), LW 51:71–72 (WA 10/3:1–5).

48. See James D. Smart, *The Strange Silence of the Bible in the Church: A Study in Hermeneutics* (Philadelphia: Westminster, 1970).

49. Wengert, *Human Freedom, Christian Righteousness*, 80–109.

first time people come to Luther worried about whether they are elect, Luther breaks with his own "right answer" by insisting (quite illogically) that were he to discover at the last judgment that he was not among the elect, he would throw his baptism in God's face![50] Nothing could undermine the comfort (i.e., effect) of the gospel. Melanchthon, who in later years could refer to Calvin sarcastically as "our Zeno" (after the founder of Stoicism), also insisted that the logic of election could not undermine God's promise to save sinners.

One particularly trenchant example of the centrality of inquiring after a doctrine's effect arose in the intra-Lutheran debate of the 1550s with Andreas Osiander and his followers over the question of justification. Osiander insisted that justification was not an imputation of God's righteousness through the Word but rather an ontological reality caused by the indwelling of Christ's divinity in the believer. Alongside all of the standard exegetical arguments and citations of Luther over the meaning of John 16 and Romans 3–4 (among others), from the very beginning writers accused Osiander of robbing believers of the comfort of the gospel, that is, the effect of the gospel, since such an indwelling was impossible to measure with certainty but God's promise remained certain no matter what.[51]

Was Christum Treibet! What Pushes Christ!

In German, the verb *treiben* (etymologically related to the English "drive") has a myriad of meanings. In the massive German dictionary, started by the brothers Grimm of fairy-tale fame, the word takes up several columns. The author of this entry even devotes a lengthy paragraph to Martin Luther's own use of the term—one that continued to echo among later German theologians.

---

50. For this "broken" view of election, see Robert Kolb, *Bound Choice, Election, and Wittenberg Theological Method: From Martin Luther to the Formula of Concord* (Grand Rapids: Eerdmans, 2005), esp. 271–90.

51. See Timothy J. Wengert, *Defending Faith: Lutheran Responses to Andreas Osiander's Doctrine of Justification* (Tübingen: Mohr Siebeck, 2012), 31.

Luther uses "*treiben*" with the meaning of "to occupy oneself with something," with a particularly active element, stating, "The apostles and Christ himself *push* [*treiben*] this wisdom, and in this manner I know of no other book of the New Testament [than Romans] in which it is *pushed*. To be sure, it is touched upon here and there but nowhere *pushed*. However, this one book of the New Testament *pushes* it continually and concentrates on it, so that it depicts for people the weak and strong Christ [cf. Romans 15:1–3]."[52] He uses it particularly in relation to preaching: "Those who rightly [*rechtschaffen*] preach and *push* Christ."[53] Peculiarly Luther: "In this all of the truly holy books agree: that they all preach and *push* Christ."[54] . . . The frequency of this way of speaking in Luther caused its continued existence, especially in theological writing into the eighteenth century.[55]

In his preface to James and Jude, written for the 1522 September Testament, Luther defines the measuring stick for all "truly holy books," and thus gives James especially a lower status in the Bible. In some ways, centering Scripture and its interpretation on Christ relates not only to the New Testament's approach to the Hebrew Scriptures and rightly defines the former's catholicity, but it also reflects Luther's commitment to reading Psalms and, hence, the entire Bible in the light of Christ, not unrelated to typology and allegory (as defined in the medieval Quadriga and elsewhere). But his use of the word *treiben* ups the ante, so to speak. What makes both Scripture and its interpretation "true" (German: *rechtschaffen*) is precisely their pushing and emphasizing Christ—and not just Christ as moral teacher (as Erasmus often did) but as Savior.[56] Thus James fails the test of apostolicity

52. WA 12:513.

53. WA 12:537.

54. WA Bi 7:386 (LW 35:396, where the word is [mistakenly] translated "inculcate"), citing Luther's preface to James and Jude. See Timothy J. Wengert, *Reading the Bible with Martin Luther: An Introductory Guide* (Grand Rapids: Baker Academic, 2013), 1–21.

55. Jacob Grimm and Wilhelm Grimm et al., eds., *Deutsches Wörterbuch* (Leipzig, 1854–1961), 22:64, https://tinyurl.com/y9gglxap. Thus the CA 26.20 (BC 76–77) uses *treiben* this way, rendered *urgere* (to urge) in the Latin.

56. Both Luther and Melanchthon often warn against making Christ into "another Moses," by which they mean simply a lawgiver. Here they are depending on John 1:17: "the law indeed was given through Moses; grace and truth came through Jesus Christ."

for Luther *not* just because of its comments about faith and works in chapter 2 but because it says very little about Christ *at all*, makes no mention of the Holy Spirit, and (in chapter 2) misinterprets Genesis. Luther's sophisticated arguments here unmask the addiction of certain authors today to placing James in the center of their exegesis and thought—where morality and human merit (not God's mercy in Christ) rule.

This means that what gives interpreters authority and what gives Scripture authority is one and the same thing: the witness to Christ. What confirms this authority is the effect God's Word has on us: unmasking our sin and redeeming the sinner, terrifying and comforting, putting to death and making alive. That is, the authorization of Scripture comes from the two aspects of the phrase *Was Christum treibet*: the content of the witness of and to Christ and its effect as it, literally, drives the sinner to Christ through law and gospel, as will be shown in chapter 3.

But lurking behind Luther's colorful word is a very different solution to the Christian problem of how to relate the two Testaments without caving in to supersessionism on the one hand or to a complete isolation of the two testaments from one another on the other. Supersessionism views the Hebrew Scriptures as a mere shadow, only important as a type or vague reference to Christ. Then the Israelites and their Jewish descendants fade into obscurity, and Christianity supersedes its Jewish forebears. Now there is no doubt that Luther often talks that way, and in his anti-Jewish tracts of 1543 he insists that large portions of the Hebrew Scriptures are simply direct prophecies of Christ. Yet certain aspects of his theology mitigate this approach, especially his discovery of the "faithful synagogue" (discussed in chap. 1) and his arguments that the Jewish people were not guilty of Christ's death but that all humanity is. With the rejection of the Quadriga, Luther gained new respect for the historical record, so that he did not simply dismiss the actual history of Israel but used it as examples of how God's word of promise made and sustained believers throughout history.

The reaction to supersessionism, already hinted at by some sixteenth-century exegetes but dominating modern and postmodern interpretation, is to sever most, if not all, connections between the two Testaments. This new "orthodoxy" was so strong that when Gerhard von Rad introduced a kind of typological interpretation pointing to Christ at the end of the second volume of his *Theology of the Old Testament*, some critics objected.[57] Sometime later, when Brevard Childs fostered a canonical reading of texts, suspicions of supersessionist tendencies arose.[58] For many exegetes, the safest way to interpret the Hebrew Scriptures is by removing all references to Christ, which inadvertently places faith in their own objectivity (or subjectivity), even for those who in fact are believers in Christ and members of a Christian church.

There is, however, another way to make the connection, one that Luke hints at in the concluding chapter of his Gospel. The language describing the disciples' reaction to the Resurrected One is often overlooked, and yet it reveals precisely the "emotional field" into which Christians may place their encounters with the Hebrews Scriptures. "They stood still, looking sad" (Luke 24:17). This sadness along with fear and disbelief characterize the emotional *Sitz im Leben* of this text. Jesus's response, too, is filled with emotion: "Oh, how foolish you are, and how slow of heart to believe *all that the prophets have declared!*" (v. 25). Their encounter with Christ is immediately an encounter with the Hebrew Scriptures, so that (v. 27) Jesus "interpreted to them the things about himself in all the scriptures." Then, of course, the breaking of bread—Christ in the worshiping community's midst with bread and wine—reveals him to these clueless fellows. Their reaction is not fact based but emotion laden (v. 32): "Were not our hearts burning within us . . . while he was opening the scriptures to us?" But the story is not over with their race back to Jerusalem. When Jesus then appears to the Eleven (plus Cleopas and his friend) and after he had proved the incarnation still obtained by downing a fish sandwich, Jesus says (v. 44), "These are my words that I spoke to you while I was still with you—that everything written about me in the law of Moses, the prophets, and the psalms must be fulfilled." And just

57. See Gerhard von Rad, *Old Testament Theology*, trans. D. M. G. Stalker (New York: Harper & Row, 1962–1965), 2:336–429.

58. Brevard Childs, *Biblical Theology in Crisis* (Philadelphia: Westminster, 1970).

so we don't miss the point, Luke adds (v. 45), "Then he opened their minds to understand the scriptures," where Jesus summarizes the heart of that understanding this way (vv. 46–47): "Thus it is written, that the Messiah is to suffer and to rise from the dead on the third day, and that repentance and forgiveness of sins is to be proclaimed in his name to all nations, beginning from Jerusalem."

Of course, when Melanchthon and other Lutherans hear "repentance and forgiveness" in one breath, they immediately understand it as law and gospel (see chap. 3). More than that, however, they connect this movement from the work of the law to that of the gospel with Jesus's own death and resurrection and, hence, with baptism. Now, taken as a whole, these resurrection stories function to sharpen Luke's approach to the Hebrew Scripture. The question of one thing "superseding" another seems quite beside the point. Everything written of Christ in the whole Scripture (Law, Prophets, and Writings) "must be fulfilled." Unfortunately, this fulfillment is often reduced, even by Luther, to a mechanical matter of obscure things in the Hebrew Scripture suddenly finding their "real" (and only!) meaning in Christ. Instead, that fulfillment is the experience of death and resurrection, that is, repentance and forgiveness.

At the same time, the blindness of the Emmaus disciples and the terror and doubts mixed with joy of the Jerusalem Eleven must not be lost from sight. The way in which Christ is the center of Scripture and in which the interpreter looks for what pushes Christ is far more the language and experience of love. When one encounters two lovers head over heels for one another, they often play a game—despite the way it bores and horrifies their friends—where they piece together the random events that led to their meeting and proclaim that it "just had to be" and that their relationship "was made in heaven." Finding Christ in the Hebrew Scriptures is just this kind of love talk—starting in the first century and continuing to this day. Like the language of predestination, the language of the unity of the testaments and *was Christum treibet* is the language of love. Standing at the cross and by the empty tomb, encountering the

Resurrected One in Word and Sacrament, is not logic but love, so that now everything looks different. No wonder Ephesians shouts at the beginning of its remarkable fourteen-verse sentence (in Greek): "He chose us in Christ before the foundation of the world. . . ." This prooftext for predestination dare never be used simply to slake one's thirst for explanation but must always be heard for the love song that it is: "There was never a time when God did not have you in mind." In light of this world of feeling, no wonder that Christian exegetes encounter Christ throughout the Hebrew Scriptures! What else is there to comfort the terrified?

Authorizing the Authors

In the sixteenth century, almost all exegetes without exception held that the Bible was the inspired Word of God.[59] Questions of *how* the Holy Spirit inspired its authors, however, garnered very little if any interest. Jacques Lefèvre d'Étaples insisted that the inspiration of the gospel writers matched the inspiration of later readers, permitting, for example, his corrections to the standard Latin translation. John Calvin was likely influenced by this argument (passed on to him either directly or through Martin Bucer), so that he could describe the biblical authors as amanuenses of the Holy Spirit and yet also stress the internal testimony of the Holy Spirit in the believing readers' hearts. Only after he separated these two parts of this argument in the final edition of the *Institutes* do we find interpreters struggling to define these two levels of inspiration apart from one another.[60]

The Roman Catholic Church also took seriously the inspiration of Scripture, setting out at the Council of Trent and for the first time in Western Christianity a definitive list of inspired books, while also insisting that other, oral traditions from Jesus and the apostles had their own authority, as passed down in the

59. For a somewhat different and more expansive discussion, see Robert Kolb, *Martin Luther and the Enduring Word of God: The Wittenberg School and Its Scripture-Centered Proclamation* (Grand Rapids: Baker Academic, 2016), 75–89, where he properly takes issue with Wengert, *Reading the Bible*.

60. Richard Muller, *The Unaccommodated Calvin: Studies in the Formation of a Theological Tradition* (New York: Oxford University Press, 2000).

church fathers, councils, and papal decrees. Of course, as the successor to St. Peter, the pope himself possessed authority to interpret Scripture to which the church granted special weight. The exact nature of this authority, however, would have to await the First Vatican Council for further definition and the Second Vatican Council for still further qualification.

The first Wittenberg exegete to examine the question of scriptural authority extensively, however, was neither Luther nor Melanchthon but rather their student Georg Major (1502–1574), a professor at Wittenberg beginning in 1545. In a tract published in 1550, Major argued for the priority of scriptural authority over against the pope and his councils, as the title of his book suggests.[61] The dedicatory epistle, addressed to Archbishop of Canterbury Thomas Cranmer, was dated July 22, 1550. This dedication, combined with the title, shows that Major's main goal was not so much to prove the inspiration of the biblical writers but to contrast Scripture's inspired authority to that of the recently convoked Council of Trent, where in 1550 negotiations were underway to invite certain evangelicals. Startling to modern readers are his initial arguments that neither the prophets nor the apostles taught anything new but simply gave witness to the incarnation of the Savior of the world, Jesus Christ. This clearly echoed Luther's *Was Christum treibet* and grounded Major's arguments in Christology.

Major introduced the heart of the first part of his book with this overview: "Therefore, in order to confirm our souls, let us propose some brief grounds that show that the Prophetic and Apostolic writings are the voice and command of the eternal God."[62] He gave nine proofs: the type of teaching (divine and not human), the effect of this teaching (which removes the hopelessness of the human situation by declaring hearers to be God's children), the consistency of this teaching over the ages

---

61. Georg Major, *A Quite Necessary Admonition, for This Time When Dealing with the Council That Has Been Called, concerning the Origin and Authority of the Word of God and What May Be the Authority of Popes, Fathers, and Councils, to Which Is Added a Catalogue of the Teachers of the Church of God from the Beginning of the World to the Present Age* (Wittenberg: J. Lufft, 1550). For the Latin original, *De origine . . .*, see the bibliography.

62. Major, *De origine*, B 4r.

(the analogy [cited in Greek as ἀναλογία] of faith), the fulfillment of prophecies (i.e., God's promises beginning with Abraham), the witness of miracles (especially mentioning the exodus,
Jericho, and Christ's miracles), the conservation of this teaching
despite the hatred of Satan, the continuity of the church from
Adam to the present, the blood of the martyrs from Abel, and
the horrible divine punishment of certain heretics.

After listing the succession of teachers in the church from
Adam to Martin Luther, Major addressed three topics: the
authority of councils, the well-known saying of Augustine ("I
would not have believed the gospel if the authority of the church
had not moved me"), and the gift of interpretation. On Augustine's statement, rather than placing the church's authority over
Scripture, Major first argued that the "catholic church," to which
Augustine refers, is obviously one that retains the basic, true
teaching of Christ. "The church has this authority of testimony,
which is able to judge between the voice of their own Shepherd
Christ and the voice of wolves, and it has it not from itself but
from God so that, indeed, the authority of the church is not
greater than that of the Word of God."[63]

On the question of the gift of interpretation, Major began this
way:

> Among the various gifts that pertain to ministers, there is the gift
> of interpretation, which is the light in faithful souls who love and
> carefully hand down the Word of God (itself divinely inflamed
> through the Holy Spirit), for the right and proper understanding of
> the heavenly teaching, for discerning the Gospel from philosophy
> and human reason, and for the uncovering and refutation of errors
> and opinions that do not conform to the Word of God.[64]

This gift was not bound to certain persons or places (e.g., to the
pope or Rome).[65] Such interpretation did not depend on human
reason but rather first on Scripture interpreting Scripture and

---

63. Major, *De origine*, G 3r–v.

64. Major, *De origine*, G 5r.

65. Luther once added that the gift of interpretation was also not bound to Wit-
tenberg and its pastor Bugenhagen. See Gordon Lathrop and Timothy J. Wengert,
Christian Assembly: Marks of the Church in a Pluralistic Age (Minneapolis: Fortress
Press, 2004), 104.

then on the universal consensus of the church, where such a consensus depended on faithful apostolic teaching and was sincerely handed down by the church and its ministers.

This tract shows just how far Major and the Wittenberg theologians were from arguing over the *nature* of inspiration. They simply assumed that the Bible was the Word of God. Even when they cite 2 Timothy 3:16 ("All Scripture is given by inspiration of God, and is profitable . . ." [KJV]), they focused on the second half of the text and its profitability, its use and impact on the hearer or reader—that is, meaning as definition and effect as described above.[66]

Although scholars generally admit that Luther never spoke about the nature of the Bible's inspiration, all admit that he, too, insisted on its inspiration. Yet on two points Luther diverged from his later followers. First, in the prefaces to the New Testament of 1522, he reopened the question of the canon, that is, which books belong in the New Testament, with the result that he placed James, Jude, and Revelation in a kind of appendix at the end of the book and questioned their authority (especially and famously that of James). Second, Luther rarely used the phrase often associated with his approach to biblical authority: *sola Scriptura* (Scripture alone).[67]

On the first issue, despite charges by later exegetes, Luther was not so much using his theology to exclude a book that did not back him up as he was using standard humanist tools to judge the nature of an ancient document. Luther knew that the ancient church fathers had already raised questions about including James in the canon. He also was following the positions raised by two of his fiercest opponents: Tommaso de Vio (Cardinal Cajetan) and Erasmus of Rotterdam. These two had also questioned James's authorship. Luther noted that James did not

66. A great example comes from Dietrich, *Summaria über die gantze Bibel*, CXLI[r]: "Here St. Paul points Timothy to his example that . . . he obtains comfort for himself in the Scripture. For the Scripture is the one true light, where we avoid offense and where such offense cannot affect us, as St. Paul says so well here. The Scripture is needful 1) for teaching, so that one can know God rightly; 2) for reproof, so that one can ward off sin; 3) for improvement, so that one comes to the forgiveness of sins; 4) for discipline, so that one keeps oneself in holy, godly way of life and be righteous."

67. For a much fuller discussion of these topics, see Wengert, *Reading the Bible*, 1–21.

contain well-constructed arguments but jumped from one thing to another, and he even proposed a literary explanation: here was a postapostolic author who, having heard what the apostles had taught, put down snatches of a variety of their sayings.

Alongside these historical arguments, Luther also made some theological observations. In James's favor, Luther insisted that, unlike Luther's own opponents who taught only human laws and works, James was indeed expounding God's law. Unfortunately, James's letter did not live up to Jesus's own definition in John 15:28 of an apostle's office: one who was to witness to Christ's death and resurrection. Instead, all he was concerned with was God's law, and he never mentioned the Holy Spirit. Moreover, in chapter 2, the author misquotes and misunderstands Genesis and Abraham, contradicting Paul.

In the standard medieval lectionary, which Luther and Lutherans otherwise assiduously followed,[68] James appeared twice, as epistle lessons during the Easter season. Luther did not understand this decision, and Wittenberg, for the most part, replaced those readings with ones from 1 Corinthians 15 on the resurrection. However, on several occasions in the 1530s, Luther even delivered sermons on the appointed texts from James—carefully rehearsing his questions about authorship and theological trustworthiness.[69]

On the second issue, *sola Scriptura*, the absence of this term in Melanchthon (he never used it!) and its rare use in Luther should raise flags for its use today to summarize Lutheran approaches to Scripture. While *sola fide* (by faith alone) occurs approximately 1,200 times, *solus Christus* about 500, and *sola gratia* 120, the catchphrase *sola Scriptura* comes up in Luther's Latin works only 18 times.[70] Of those eighteen, nine are places where Luther explicitly says he will not argue *sola Scriptura* (from Scripture

68. Unlike more recent Lutherans (under the influence of certain Reformed views of Scripture), Luther did not think he had the authority to do away with the lectionary and praised it for treating Christ's incarnation, death, and resurrection for half the year.

69. Timothy J. Wengert, "Building on the One Foundation with Straw: Martin Luther and the Epistle of James," *Word and World* 35 (2015): 251–61.

70. See Timothy J. Wengert, "A Note on 'Sola Scriptura' in Martin Luther's Writings," *Luther-Bulletin* 20 (2011): 21–31; Wengert, *Reading the Bible*, 16–21. Two other occurrences from the Weimar edition of Luther's works online are descriptions

alone). This leaves only nine passages, all of which refer to arguments against papal hegemony over the interpretation of Scripture, the same argument found in Major's tract.

Peter Fraenkel, the Melanchthon scholar who taught for years at the University of Geneva, proposes a much better phrase to describe Melanchthon's view of Scripture—one that could also be used for Luther.[71] The Bible's authority is *primum et verum*, the first and true authority. Later Lutherans echo similar thoughts when they distinguish two types of authority in theology. Scripture is the *norma normans* (the norm norming [all other norms]); every other authority is a *norma normata* (a norm normed [by Scripture]). For this second kind of authority, Melanchthon referred to the church fathers especially as testimonies or witnesses, who point away from themselves (like John the Baptist in John 1) and toward the "Lamb of God who takes away the sin of the world."[72] For this reason, Lukas Cranach Sr. and his son often depicted Luther in the pulpit pointing his rapt listeners to the Lamb of God. The creeds and confessions of the church (as well as the writings of the fathers, Luther, Melanchthon, and others) received their authority from the one to whom they witness.[73] In this, they run parallel to the witness of the apostles and prophets. Without this second witness, the "first and true" witness could well remain trapped in history, unable to do the very thing for which God appointed it.

In his battles with opponents he labels Sacramentarians or ravers (German: *Schwärmer*), Luther confronted a further problem related to inspiration of Scripture. People like Andreas Bodenstein (Karlstadt) pointed to Old Testament commands regarding Jubilee years, images, and tithing, insisting that because they were in God's word Christians should follow them.

of his opponents (again Erasmus and Cajetan) who offered to argue with Luther using Scripture alone.

71. Peter Fraenkel, *Testimonia Patrum: The Function of the Patristic Argument in the Theology of Philip Melanchthon* (Geneva: Droz, 1961).

72. See CA 20.12 (Latin), in BC 55.

73. See Kolb, *Enduring Word of God*, 85, where he mentions other authorities as being "at best" secondary. This devalues the actual witness of the church and its teachers (including Luther). They were secondary in that they were the Holy Spirit's instrumental witnesses that continue to enliven the church through God's Word down through the ages.

Luther, while accepting the fact that they are truly God's word, demands that readers ask a second question: "Are they God's Word for God's people today?" This insistence that Scripture's authority depends in some way on the historical and literary context further undermines any attempts to reduce Wittenberg's exegesis to a kind of nascent fundamentalism. Luther writes,

> One must deal cleanly with the Scriptures. From the very beginning the word has come to us in various ways. It is not enough simply to look and see whether this is God's word, whether God has spoken it; rather we must look and see to whom it has been spoken, whether it fits us. That makes all the difference between night and day. . . . The word in Scripture is of two kinds: the first does not pertain or apply to me, the other kind does. . . . The false prophets pitch in and say, "Dear people, this is the word of God." This is true; we cannot deny it. But we are not "that people."[74]

Luther's Meditative Exegesis

As we will read in chapter 5, Luther reflected on his method of biblical interpretation (and thus his approach to theology) in the 1539 preface to his German works.[75] There, using Latin terms associated with the monastic *lectio divina*, he argued that true theology is a matter of reading Scripture through prayer, meditation, and struggle (*oratio, meditatio,* and *tentatio*).[76] One begins with prayer because human wisdom cannot fathom Scripture's meaning. Then, one meditates—by which Luther means not using a mantra to be catapulted into some "cloud cuckoo land" but taking care to examine each individual word and asking, "Whatever could the Holy Spirit have meant by that?" Finally, once prayer and meditation have overturned reason and made

---

74. LW 35: 170, with minor corrections. For a lengthier discussion, see Wengert, *Reading the Bible*, 34.

75. See below, pp. 146–49. For a modern use of these categories, see Oswald Bayer, *Theology the Lutheran Way*, ed. and trans. Jeffrey G. Silcock and Mark C. Mattes (Grand Rapids: Eerdmans, 2007).

76. Luther drops *lectio* (reading) and folds it into *meditatio* (meditation) but now without certain aspects of the mystical experience. He replaces *contemplatio* (contemplation) with the far more radical *tentatio*, which he relates to the actual, living experience of the reader.

the reader dependent on the work of God's Spirit, all hell breaks loose, and the theologian discovers himself or herself in the midst of *Anfechtung*, that is, attack or assault from the devil, the world, and the flesh.

Luther's discursive style of biblical interpretation rests on this monastic basis and leads him to use several different aspects of the exegetical method championed by humanists as well. He begins with the individual words and finds himself continually surprised by what he finds there. He thus uses his knowledge of Greek and Hebrew to enrich his *meditatio*. He also loves to use paraphrase—not only in sermons but also in his major exegetical lectures. He may begin with a traditional introduction to paraphrase, "It is as if Paul [or Jesus or Moses] were saying. . . ." But these paraphrases go beyond simply stating the text using other words and get far more into the emotional world of the text so that it directly addresses Luther's hearers and Luther himself. Moreover, he can also use this form of direct address to allow God to come to voice. Thus a reference in Galatians, say, to Christ being a curse for us can become for Luther a discussion of what God is actually saying to Christ on the cross, as he becomes at God's command a variety of biblical sinners. The vividness of Luther's exegetical imagination is unparalleled in the sixteenth century and results in a far livelier experience of the text for the reader.[77]

Foolish Truth-Telling

There is one more aspect of the combination of fact and effect that helps define Wittenberg's biblical interpretation: the theology of the cross. This theology is not a theory of the atonement, as its name might imply, but rather, based on 1 Corinthians 1:18–25, the revelation of God in the last place human beings would reasonably look: in the foolishness and weakness of the biblical story. Although Martin Luther used the term itself or its equivalent only rarely,[78] it shaped his entire theology.

---

77. For an analysis of a portion of Luther's Galatians lectures and commentaries, see Wengert, *Reading the Bible*, 92–122.

78. Heidelberg Disputation (1518; AL 1:98–101 [WA 1:361–63]); *Explanation of*

The biblical texts and stories constantly surprise Luther, saying the very opposite of what especially the hyper-religious of his day assumed. For example, where Luke mentions that the shepherds return to their flocks, Luther notes,

> All walks of life, whatever they may be, receive their origin from God and, living in them, a person can be a Christian, in a way that they may appropriately use them. For the evangelist does not write, "The shepherds left their office to enter a monastery and profess that they were chaste, so that they might initiate a godly and Christian life . . . ," but he says that the shepherds went back to their flocks and cattle, where they served their calling.[79]

The theology of the cross may also assist Christians with the question of Scripture's authority. Claims of inerrancy and infallibility—however helpful they may seem for shoring up Scripture's authority and faith's certainty—come a cropper precisely on Paul's words in 1 Corinthians 1:21: "through the foolishness of our proclamation." Part of this foolishness attacks our penchant for claiming that our reason and wisdom can penetrate the mystery of God's work in the world. Yet the Bible presents a foolish picture throughout: the God of creation with dirt under fingernails in Genesis 2; the God of Exodus choosing the weak, "mixed multitude" of Israelites rather than the strong Egyptians; the God of Jerusalem's last days choosing weak Jeremiah. And then, of course, there is a foolish birth, life, and death of the Messiah. The opponents are wise when they ask, "Can anything good come out of Nazareth?" (John 1:46), or when they cry, "Who are you, Jesus of Nazareth . . . ?" (see Mark 1:24), and "If you are the Son of God . . . come down from the cross"

---

the 95 Theses (1518; LW 31:128–30; 224–28 [WA 1:557–58; 612–14]); Bondage of the Will (1525; LW 33:62 [WA 18:633], where he uses the concept but not the term). Other occurrences (all from 1518) include the Asterisci Lutheri adversus Obeliscos Eckii (1518; WA 1:289, 20–291, 31); the Lectures on Hebrews (1518; WA 57/3:79–81; LW 27:XX). See also a comment from 1519 in the Operationes in Psalmos (WA 5:300). A comment on Ps 126:5 from 1532/1533 refers to the theology of the cross as well (WA 40/3:193, 4–8). I am indebted to Irving Sandberg for these citations.

79. WA 34/2:565, 17–21, from a sermon delivered in 1531. He consistently interpreted this text in this way. See also WA 37:246 (sermon from 1533) and WA 10/1/1:137–38 (the Christmas Postil of 1522).

(Matt 27:40). Bad enough that the Messiah is crucified, but his followers are also no great shakes either: children, women, and the foolish, fickle, denying, betraying, abandoning Twelve. No wonder in 1 Corinthians 1:25–31, Paul turns to his audience and insists that they are not such great shakes either! And Paul himself (1 Cor 2:1–4) comes with fear and trembling, and later in 2 Corinthians 12:9–10, "So, I will boast all the more gladly of my weaknesses, so that the power of Christ may dwell in me . . . for whenever I am weak, then I am strong." Thus only when the Scripture, the interpreter, and the hearer are weak are they then strong.

Melanchthon's training in rhetoric led him to categorize paradox as a rhetorical tool (rather than a dialectical one). Thus he did not ever refer directly to the theology of the cross. Regarding ecclesiology, however, he insisted that the church's outward appearance fooled people into missing the fact that God's church always exists among the lowest people (Mary, Joseph, shepherds, Elizabeth, and Zechariah) and that therefore the outward pomp and power of the Roman opponents should not trick readers into imagining that the former and not Wittenberg were the true church. He also occasionally developed what might be called a pedagogy of the cross, once again emphasizing the weakness of the gospel over against human wisdom.[80]

A splendid example of a later Wittenberg exegete who makes use of the same categories comes from Joachim Mörlin, a late student of Luther often nicknamed "Luther's chaplain." As pastor at the main church in Königsberg, Mörlin was one of the most important early opponents of Andreas Osiander, who accused him of denigrating the Trinity in a Christmas Day sermon. In his defense, Mörlin echoed in his sermon on John 1:14,

> To this extent I confess now just as I also confessed then, that I did not only preach that we do not *know* what God is *in God's essence*—let alone try to discuss and talk about it (as Gregory of Nazianzus, Augustine, Ambrose and Hilary[81] also write)—but I

---

80. Timothy J. Wengert, "Caspar Cruciger Sr.'s 1546 'Enarratio' on John's Gospel: An Experiment in Ecclesiological Exegesis," *Church History* 61 (1992): 60–74.

81. Teachers and bishops of the ancient church, active in the fourth and fifth centuries.

said even more. The Scripture also talks very little about who God is in God's very self, namely, God the Father, Son and Holy Spirit. Instead, it talks for the most part about what God is for us: namely God is merciful, who lets our misery abate and moves us gently, who suffers with us and takes upon himself such misery. Thus, I defend myself from raving speculators as from the devil—those who want to interpret absolutely words with relational meanings that refer to specific contexts. Thus, for them, the righteousness of God becomes that by which God is righteous in God's very being. Watch out! Or, flee to the Bible, which shows our dear God wearing baby shoes [*Kinderschuhen*] and draws God out of that heavenly essence (within which God can never be understood in this life) to be among us, in that God speaks, has eyes, ears, hands, feet, which God actually does not have. Not, I say, in God's divine essence, as God is in God's very self from all eternity, but instead as God came into the world and walked among us. Oh my! Look at how John makes himself happy and is filled with joy about this and says, "We have also seen the glory of the only begotten Son." Where is that, dear John, where is that? "He is lying in a manger, has hands and feet, body and soul," that is, "The Word became flesh."[82]

LUTHERAN EXEGESIS TODAY

In addition to the distinction of law and gospel (see chap. 3), the conscious blending of definition and effect provide a stark contrast to many approaches to Scripture current today. For one thing, one cannot simply ask what it meant in one place before asking, What does it mean? in another. Instead, the interpreter and the reader or hearer of the interpretation become immediately caught up in a text, so that the experience of biblical interpretation does not begin with the exegete or the recipient of exegesis but rather with the text itself and what it is doing to the one reading. The scandal of the text, of God *sub contrario specie*, does something to the reader. In that very activity the reader is driven to the Crucified, so that *Was Christum treibet* also drives the reader. At the same time, this experience of the text itself creates and strengthens the text's authority. Here the Latin root

82. Joachim Mörlin, *Historia Welcher gestalt sich die Osiandrische schwermerey im lande zu Preussen erhaben, vnd wie dieselbige verhandelt ist, mit allen actis beschrieben* ([Magdeburg: Michael Lotter], 1554), R 3^{v}–R 4^{r}.

word *auctoritas* may help broaden what authority means in this connection: not simply might and power but more accurately (*sub contrario specie*) a producing or increase or even encouragement, from which the Bible's dignity and influence arise and through which its credibility may be established. Without this blending of fact and effect, the authority of the Bible is but a clanging bell or an empty cymbal.

3.

The Law Always Accuses; The Gospel Always Forgives

Words can have a myriad of effects on a listener: they can entertain, bore, frighten, soothe, inform, anger—the list could go on and on! What Luther and Melanchthon noticed was that the Word of God had two basic effects, which they and their successors summarized with the terms "law" and "gospel." In his early lectures on Psalms and Romans, Luther used the traditional, Augustinian distinction of letter and spirit, but this quickly changed as he expanded his search for the Word's effect beyond 2 Corinthians 3:6 ("The letter kills, but the Spirit gives life") to other Pauline texts. For one thing, he and his colleagues noticed that Paul himself described the function of God's law in several important passages. Romans 3:20: "through the law comes the knowledge of sin." Galatians 2:19, 21: "For through the law I died to the law, so that I might live to God. . . . I do not nullify the grace of God; for if justification comes through the law, then Christ died for nothing." Romans 4:14–15: "If it is the adherents of the law who are to be the heirs, faith is null and the promise is void. For the law brings wrath."

Alongside the law, which works to reveal sin, bring wrath and terror, and put to death, comes a second Word of God, the gospel. Indeed, in this context law and gospel work as a matched pair. Calling this second word *gospel* comes directly from Romans 1:16–17: "For I am not ashamed of the gospel; it is the power of God for salvation to everyone who has faith, to the Jew first and also to the Greek. For in it the righteousness of God is revealed through faith for faith; as it is written, 'The one who is righteous will live by faith.'" The Reformers insist that the gospel is not simply information about Christ but includes all of the promises of God and that these promises work on human beings to make them believers. Thus the gospel reveals the Savior, brings forgiveness and comfort, and makes alive.

In article 20 of the Augsburg Confession, Melanchthon tied the effect of the gospel to Romans 5:1 ("Therefore, since we are justified by faith, we have peace with God through our Lord Jesus Christ"), a point made explicit in his 1532 Romans commentary. Luther linked the work of law and gospel to the Word of God in baptism, through which the old creature is drowned and the new creature of faith is raised up to life. This daily drowning and rising comes to expression in the sacrament of absolution, which is nothing other than a return to one's baptism. Hence, in the Augsburg Confession, the effects of law and gospel first appear in article 12, *de poenitentia* (translated "on repentance, penitence, or penance"). "Now properly speaking, true *poenitentia* is nothing else than to have contrition and sorrow, or terror about sin and yet at the same time to believe in the gospel and absolution that sin is forgiven and grace is obtained through Christ. Such faith, in turn, comforts the heart and puts it at peace."[1]

In his defense of this article in the Apology, Melanchthon defines law and gospel this way:

> For these are the two chief works of God in human beings, to justify the terrified or make them alive. The entire Scripture is divided into these two works. One part is the law, which reveals, denounces, and condemns sin. The second part is the gospel, that is, the promise of grace given in Christ. This promise is constantly repeated throughout the entire Scripture: first it was given to Adam, later to the patriarchs, then illuminated by the prophets, and finally proclaimed and offered by Christ among the Jews, and spread throughout the entire world by the apostles. For all

1. CA 12.3–5, in BC 44.

the saints have been justified by faith in this promise and not on account of their own attrition or contrition.[2]

In the paragraphs that follow, Melanchthon (who had already demonstrated this twofold movement from judgment to grace with countless Bible passages) provided not more prooftexts but examples from Scripture. In Genesis 3 the couple flees from God (law) and then hears God's promise of the snake's defeat. In 2 Samuel 12:13 David, having been condemned by Nathan, shows true repentance (the work of the law) and receives absolution (the gospel). Similarly, the woman who anoints Jesus's feet in Luke 7 comes to him in tears (contrition worked by the law) and receives forgiveness because of her faith (worked by Jesus's promise).

Luther began to use the terms "law" and "gospel" (or "commands" and "promises") quite early in the Reformation, with one of his most important early expositions coming in the 1520 tract *Freedom of a Christian*.[3] There, in two separate places, he outlined what the law is (God's commands) and what the gospel is (God's promises) but then went on to describe primarily their effect of revealing sin and creating faith. Even before introducing these categories, in the very first paragraph of the Latin edition, which forms a kind of exordium to the entire tract, Luther criticized those who imagine faith is a virtue (thus something human beings can work on to create or improve) and insisted that it is only known through experience. This experience, as he then showed later, is precisely the experience of hearing the Word of God (since Paul insists that "faith comes from what is heard" [Rom 10:17]). For this reason Luther ended the first main section of his work by describing, in order, bad preaching, good preaching, and good preaching's effects.[4] Bad preaching either simply tells the story of Jesus, focuses on laws for people to fulfill, or plays on their emotions. Good preaching proclaims that this Christ is "for you" and brings about comfort and joy.[5]

2. Ap 12.53, in BC 195.

3. See AL 1:466–538, esp. 494–96 (WA 7:39–73, esp. 52–53).

4. AL 1:508–9 (WA 7:58–59).

5. This is so much a part of Protestant exegesis and theology that it is no accident that the sixteenth- or seventeenth-century English Christmas carol proclaims Christ's birth as "tidings of comfort and joy."

One of the most interesting examples of the work of law and gospel in Scripture, not mentioned by the Reformers, comes in Mark 10:17–31, where the rich man approaches Jesus: "Good teacher, what must I do to inherit eternal life?" The initial response of Jesus is a great example of Markan irony: "Why do you call me good? No one is good but God alone" (v. 18). Not only do Jesus's words reveal the man's hidden, judgmental view of human beings, it also contains a joke for the reader of Mark, who already knows from Mark 1:1 that the book is the gospel (good news) of Jesus Christ, *Son of God*. Jesus is not just a nice rabbi; he is good because he is God's beloved Son. In the same way, the man's question reveals our addiction to deeds. We want desperately to justify ourselves, so we ask "What must I do?" Jesus in Mark gives a stunning christological retort: "Why call me good?"[6]

Jesus then proceeds to preach the law to the man, using the "second table" of the Ten Commandments (from honoring parents through false witness). Of course, Lutherans may wonder how the man could claim to have kept them, but Jesus lets his view of these commands stand. (After all, the broader view of the commandments comes from Matthew's Sermon on the Mount, which is lacking in Mark.) Instead he looks at the man with love.

Before finishing with Mark's story, it is important to note that Luther and Melanchthon connect this work of God in law and gospel to Isaiah 28:21, employing the terms *opus alienum* (a work alien to God's nature) and *opus proprium* (a work proper to God's nature). In Apology 12, Melanchthon writes,

> Also Isaiah 28[:21], "For the Lord will rise up as on Mount Per-azim, he will rage as in the valley of Gibeon; to do his deed—strange is his deed!—and to work his work—alien is his work!" He calls it an alien work of God to terrify, because the

6. The other Gospel writers also contrast our quest for doing religious things to faith in Jesus. John 6:25–41 contrasts the crowd working for what perishes with the Son of Man giving what endures, and then contrasts the crowd's demand to do something with "the work of God" (a subjective genitive). The same contrast appears in Luke 10:25–37, which hints at the same question ("What must I do?") but answers it with the parable of the good Samaritan—where we end up helpless in the ditch. The question also arises in John 3:1–15 and in Acts 2. In all of these texts, our questions about works are swallowed up by God's unconditional mercy in Christ. (Thanks to Irving Sandberg for these additional references.)

proper work of God is to make alive and console. But he terrifies, he says, in order to make room for consolation and vivification because hearts that do not feel the wrath of God loathe consolation in their smugness. In this way, Scripture makes a practice of joining these two things, terrors and consolation, in order to teach that these are the chief parts of repentance: contrition and faith that consoles and justifies.[7]

In the story from Mark 10, Jesus's condemnation is an alien work, which, while done out of love, is hidden. Forgiveness then is God's proper work.

The one thing lacking from this rich man is *not* generosity but faith. He is breaking the first commandment by having made wealth into an idol. Those who simply read this story as a condemnation of avarice (the love of money) may miss the point. Jesus's word of law and judgment reveals what this man trusts. He cannot follow Jesus because he cannot believe in anything but himself and his wealth. Of course, the disciples (like the rich man) adhere to a kind of prosperity gospel, which insists that the more material wealth a person has, the more God has blessed them and, hence, the closer they are to God. This idolatry of riches is the most devastating (American) heresy too. So in Mark 10:23 Jesus begins now to preach the law to the disciples (the rich man having left the scene). "How hard it will be for those who have wealth to enter the kingdom of God!" The disciples, assuming that the richer you are the nearer you are to God, are perplexed. Yet the law does not simply create perplexity; it drives to despair. So Jesus turns up the heat, so to speak. "Children [again a word revealing his heart of love despite doing this alien work], how hard it is to enter the kingdom of God! It is easier for a camel to go through the eye of a needle than for someone who is rich to enter the kingdom of God" (vv. 24–25).

Of course, here biblical commentators (like the disciples) could not believe their eyes. So somewhere along the line, someone came up with the idea of the "Eye of a Needle" Gate in Jerusalem, which was too narrow for a camel to fit in. Of course, we are so devious as to imagine that if we put the camel on a diet, greased the walls of the gate, got a strong rope and a group

7. Ap 12.51–52, in BC 195.

of really strong men, we might just squeeze the camel in. But Jesus's example is far more radical—even if such a gate existed. We are talking about a huge camel and a very tiny needle.[8] No wonder the apostles' perplexity turns to great astonishment. The law, as Jesus has been preaching it, leads them to cry out: "Then who can be saved?" (v. 26). Who indeed? The answer, as expressed by Jesus, is no one. "For mortals it is impossible" (v. 27). Now the law has done its work. The "lest anyone should boast" of Romans and Galatians has been fulfilled. Rich and poor alike are struck down by this law-filled parable: No one can be saved!

Finally, after the law has done its work, Jesus comes to the gospel: "but not for God; for God all things are possible." The only other place in the New Testament where this phrase occurs is in Luke 1:37, where the angel Gabriel reminds a doubting Mary, "For nothing will be impossible with God"—not even old Elizabeth being six months pregnant or a virgin bearing the Son of God. Thus "gospel" is always about God doing impossible things: coming in the flesh; forgiving rich and poor sinners alike.

What follows from the gospel, both in Luke 1 and in Mark 10, are confessions of faith. Mary says (Luke 1:38): "Here am I, the servant of the Lord; let it be with me according to your word." In Mark 10 the confession of faith, coming from Peter's lips, is often misconstrued as boasting about works. What matters is the tone with which we read Peter's words: not arrogantly but still amazed. "Look [or, in plain English, 'Holy moly, Lord'], we have left everything and followed you" (v. 28). Who knew how much that pleases God? And to such believers Jesus gives the promise of a hundredfold increase in houses and family (still true for the billion-plus members of Christ's body throughout the world) "with persecutions."

8. Someone claimed to me when I made this point that the "camel" was referring simply to camel's hair, which is too coarse to fit through a needle. Either way, with a gate or just the camel's hair, the impossibility of the comparison is lost on the hearers.

THE LAW'S THEOLOGICAL USE (BY GOD ON US)

In the defense of justification by faith in the Apology of the Augsburg Confession, Melanchthon wrote these often-quoted (and often-misunderstood) words: *Lex semper accusat* (the law always accuses).[9] Taken as an ontological description, the phrase can lead to all manner of misunderstandings: that the law is eternal and determines God's behavior; that faith itself is subject to the law and works; that the Lutheran approach to law is one more proof of the "introspective conscience of the West."[10] But Melanchthon was describing not a hidden metaphysics but human experience. Thus he expressed one of the central insights of the Reformation concerning the interpretation of Scripture.

To place the law within its proper exegetical context, we must begin with Luther's famous line from his first lectures on Romans—one that he continued to use throughout his career—that the human being is *simul iustus et peccator* (at the same time a righteous person and a sinner). Although he uses it in a variety of exegetical situations, Luther clearly connected his approach to an interpretation of Romans 7 that he shared with Augustine: "I do not do the good I want, but the evil I do not want is what I do" (v. 19). Luther and Augustine insisted that Romans 7 was describing Paul's life of faith and *not* his life before conversion. Indeed, before his Damascus road experience, Paul was happily a Pharisee and thus (Phil 3:6) "as to righteousness under the law, blameless." He had no problem fulfilling the law, since that was his main occupation and included overt persecution of Christians. First as a Christian, justified by faith alone, does Paul discover this raging battle between faith

9. Ap 4.38, in BC 126: "Paul says [Rom 4:15]: 'The law brings wrath.' He does not say that through the law people merit the forgiveness of sins. For the law always accuses and terrifies consciences. Therefore it does not justify since the conscience that is terrified by the law flees the judgment of God. They err, therefore, who trust that they merit the forgiveness of sins through the law and through their own works."

10. This inept formulation by Krister Stendahl, "The Apostle Paul and the Introspective Conscience of the West," *Harvard Theological Review* 56 (1963): 199–215, confuses later Lutheran pietism with Luther and Melanchthon and has become the stock excuse among adherents to the "new perspectives on Paul" to ignore and reject Lutheran interpretations of Paul and Scripture.

and law. Moreover, Paul's problem was not with ceremonial law (e.g., circumcision) but with the whole law, which is why the specific law referred to in Romans 7 is coveting, a commandment that gets to the heart of the problem or, rather, to the problem of the heart.

For Luther, the point of the *simul* was never to give an excuse to sin, as some people wrongly imagine. If it were, then the unbeliever in us could laugh at the law's condemnation, saying: "Oh, I sinned? Ha, ha, ha! Oh, well, I'm '*simul iustus et peccator*,' so it's not my fault. To err is human!" For Luther, to be a sinner is to have no claim to make before God and to have no access to God's mercy through works or rewards. It is the confession of helplessness before God, mirrored in Romans 7:24, when Paul bursts out, "Who will rescue me from this body of death?" As we saw above, in Mark 10:23–26 the disciples themselves express this helplessness, when Jesus uncovers their addiction to a prosperity gospel, which assumed that because the rich are clearly more blessed by God they are closer to God's kingdom. "Then who can be saved?" It is the same reaction found in the crowd at Pentecost in Acts 2, when Peter's preaching cuts them to the heart for crucifying God's Messiah: "What should we do?" (v. 37). David's being convicted by Nathan and Job's being convicted by the sorrows of life (and the utter uselessness of his friends' advice) also depict this sinful state. Even that first couple in the garden, running from God (or, Luther observes, from the wind rustling the leaves) because they knew they were naked, show their abject vulnerability (so that, to rephrase Luther, they were "at the same time naked and clothed").

Of course, only a handful of theology students ever heard Luther's Romans lectures in 1515–1516, although Melanchthon, who arrived in Wittenberg in 1518, seems to have had access to the manuscript for his own lectures on Romans from 1520 to 1521. Thus the *simul iustus et peccator* first burst onto the public scene in the Ninety-Five Theses, where in the very first thesis Luther summarized Jesus's preaching this way: "Our Lord and Master Jesus Christ, in saying 'Do penance . . . ,' wanted the entire life of the faithful to be one of penitence."[11] At first glance, this thesis may not seem very hermeneutically charged. After all, Luther simply cites the Vulgate, which read in Matthew 4:17: *Poenitentiam agite* (literally "do penance") and could thus be attached to the sacrament of penance. In his *Explanations of the Ninety-Five Theses*, published a year later in 1518, Luther reveals the source for this thesis: the Greek text of the New Testament where, as Erasmus of Rotterdam had pointed out in his separate book *Annotations on the New Testament*, correcting the standard Latin text, the verb *metanoiete* does not have anything to do with the sacrament of penance but with a change of mind or heart.

But Luther went far beyond Erasmus's notes on the superior Greek text by the inclusion of a single word to thesis 1: "entire." The *entire* life of the faithful is one of penitence. This profound insight into human nature directly affects how we read biblical texts and their relation to the sinner. To be sure, this radical approach has yet to penetrate most exegetes (conservative or liberal) because it destroys the notion that there is a before-and-after to the Christian life, in which one can say, "I used to be a sinner, but now that I've committed my life to Jesus I am righteous and saved." Or, "I used to be a fundamentalist, but now I follow Jesus and care for the poor." Or, as in Luther's day, when scholastic theologians all insisted that the sacrament of penance infused a person with a disposition of love, "I used to be in a state of sin, but now I am in a state of grace." Although these scholastics insisted that the material of sin (concupiscence) still clung to the justified believer, they claimed that it was not really sin until a person moved back into a state of sin by committing a wrongful act of thought, word, or deed. Moreover, scholastic theologians also insisted on distinguishing commandments, which all Christians must obey, from New Testament counsels, especially poverty, chastity, and obedience, which defined special works of supererogation that only those under a vow (monks, nuns, and friars) could fulfill for higher reward from God. Such people were in a "state of perfection," not perfect in themselves but

---

11. Timothy J. Wengert, "The 95 Theses as Luther's Template for Reading Scripture," *Lutheran Quarterly* 31 (2017): 249–66.

capable of producing far more meritorious works, where even one's sins were less powerful.

By insisting that the "entire life" of a Christian is one of penitence, Luther was also undermining the basic premise of the practice of indulgences: that by purchasing a letter of indulgence the sinner, who owed God works that chastised and disciplined the flesh, was now free from the constant rebuke of the law and its consequences. On the contrary, Luther argued, one cannot buy one's way out of the law's condemnation. Instead, one always stands before God as a sinner. In other words, when Jesus commanded his hearers, "Repent," he meant that there is never a time in the life of the faithful when that very commandment does not apply.

Our addiction to "before-and-after" theology gets to the heart of the human condition and its penchant for wanting to stay in control of one's relation to God by twisting the law so that it no longer applies to us. In the words of the well-known American hymn: "A prisoner *was* I and a-wandering, in the dark night of sin I *did* roam, then Jesus the Good Shepherd found me, and now I *am* on my way home." It is the past tense that reveals the pull of the before-and-after. "I *once* was blind, but now I see." Really? So you are not blind any longer? How does that match Jesus's deeply paradoxical condemnation of the Pharisees in John 9:41: "But now that you say, 'we see,' your sin remains"? Against such shenanigans perpetrated by the old, self-assured creature to get out from under the law, Luther insists that the *entire* life of the faithful is one of penitence. One cannot wake up some morning and decide that Jesus's stern command ("Repent!") no longer applies directly.

This insight also does not lead to introspection, as if there were only some (small) part of us that still needs fixing with repentance. The law *always* accuses, no matter how a person may feel about it, and all the self-chosen spirituality (Col 2:23) in the world cannot get us out from under this basic hermeneutical truth. We are truly sinners—not just that we confess we are sinners or that we feel shame and guilt, but that we really *are* sinners. We are always looking out for ourselves; we always need to control our relationship to God. *That* problem never goes away.

Luther's insistence that the entire life of the believer is one of penitence (that is, that we are *simul iustus et peccator*) completely changes how we interpret the Bible or, rather, how the Bible interprets us. There can no longer be *any* appeals for us to improve our standing before God. The word of the law always applies, always drives us to death ("through the law comes the knowledge of sin," Rom 3:20). Even in Galatians 2:19 ("through the law I died to the law"), the past tense should not throw us, because one can never wake up some morning when that sentence is finally passé, which is why Paul adds that he has been crucified with Christ so that "it is no longer I who live, but it is Christ who lives in me." The "I" must die—daily! Why? Because the *entire* life of the faithful is one of penitence!

This is why early on in the Reformation (by 1519) Luther rediscovered baptism—not as a gentle washing away of the smudges of sin but as a daily drowning of the old creature and raising of the new creature of faith (not works). Baptism, not as a ritual receding into the past but as a daily occurrence, provides precisely the hermeneutical key to the entire Scripture. No longer does one dare ask, "What must I *do* to inherit eternal life?" and expect a saving answer from a *good* teacher (Mark 10:17–18). As we saw above in the story of the rich young ruler, the law never ends. When he claims (perhaps rightly) that "I have kept all these [commandments] since my youth," Jesus's loving response is, "Oops! You missed one commandment (namely, the first). Go, sell everything, give to the poor, and follow me." Suddenly the "good teacher" becomes a merciless judge, and the man leaves sorrowing over his enormous wealth. But to the disciples, who also supported a form of prosperity gospel, Jesus mercilessly insisted that getting a rich person into heaven is like getting a camel through the eye of a needle. Finally, the law continued to work on these poor, benighted souls right to its (and their) alien end: "Then who can be saved?" To this the merciful, merciless judge responds: "No one! With mortals it is impossible!" The *entire* life of the faithful is one of penitence.

And penitence itself is not merely shedding crocodile tears over one's sin, as if just being sorry enough will do the trick.

Even the tax collector in Luke 18 does not say, "God, be merciful to me because I am so contrite, so sorry for my sin." Instead, he simply confesses the truth (however bad he may or may not have felt): "God, be merciful to me, a sinner" (v. 13). That *Kyrie, eleison* of Mark 10 marks the entire prayer life of the Christian church but not as proof of inward sorrow; it is simply a confession of the truth of the matter, with no reference to how remorseful one may feel. No wonder the tax collector does not "look up to heaven" (Luke 18:13)! He has no claim to make *at all.*

Another text that often evokes a "before-and-after" hermeneutic comes in Mark 8 and Matthew 16. First, Peter becomes the hero for getting the right answer, which is why in Matthew Jesus reminds Peter (and us), "Flesh and blood has not revealed this to you, but my Father in heaven" (Matt 16:17). But then comes Jesus's description of the Christian life: "If any want to become my followers, let them deny themselves . . ." (v. 24). How's that going for you? If Christianity is a matter of once being a sinner and then becoming righteous, then it is perfectly normal for us to work on our self-denial. "First, I'll give up whale meat for Lent and give a little more to world hunger and then . . ." No matter how long the list or impressive the denials, the denial of self always remains just beyond our reach. Think of it! "I, Timothy John, do hereby deny myself!" Except for this one small thing: the self is denying itself and thus, ipso facto, is not and cannot be denying itself. Thus, without even getting to the problem of "taking up the cross" (which, of course, we hope is made of balsa wood) or "following Jesus," the text becomes a permanent impossibility—until its very impossibility kills the self.

This conundrum touches on one of the most curious debates of the Reformation: Whether God commanded things that were impossible to carry out. Already Jerome in the fourth century had declared that claim heretical. As a result, when Wittenberg's Reformers began to insist that the law was not a way to heaven but a revelation of sin, their opponents insisted that they were contradicting Jerome and the entire church. As Melanchthon noted to his attackers, however, Jerome insisted that God's commands could be fulfilled only through the Holy Spirit. Without the grace of God, all commands are equally impossible, especially since they all relate back to the first commandment ("You shall have no other gods") or, as Jesus summarizes it in Mark 12:30, "You shall love the Lord your God with *all* your heart, and with *all* your soul, and with *all* your mind, and with *all* your strength." How are you doing with that? The commandment's very impossibility on its face (*all* repeated four times, just so you cannot avoid it) points to an entirely different way of hearing texts: not as doable imperatives telling us what we must believe, do, and hope for (à la the medieval Quadriga) but as absolute impossibilities that drive us to cry out with Paul (Rom 7:24), "Who will rescue me from this body of death?" Then only God the Father through the Son by the power of the Holy Spirit can rescue us—not just once but daily.

Luther's destruction of the before-and-after also results in a completely different approach to evangelism. Read or listen to any professional "evangelist" today—from the anxious bench of Charles Finney, to the methods of Dwight Moody, to the crusades (an unfortunate term) of Billy Graham and beyond—and the notion of moving people from sin to righteousness looms large and always implies that at one time the speaker/evangelist was a sinner but now has become a (righteous) Christian. Of course, quite often this approach leads to awful examples of hypocrisy (and thus has contributed to the slow demise of the Christian church in the West). But besides that, such approaches imply that the speaker is somehow different from the hearer—somehow better. Underneath always lurks the Pharisee ("I thank you God that I am no longer like that sinner over there" or "I *once* was blind").

One of the most obvious examples of Luther breaking this stranglehold of before-and-after on the commandments comes in, of all places, the *Small Catechism*. In general, the explanations to the commandments, creed, Lord's Prayer, and sacraments are paraphrastic (a favorite mode of instruction in the Renaissance), introduced with the question, "What is this?" which invited paraphrase and should best be translated: "That is to say" or "In other words." Explanations to the creed and Lord's Prayer follow this method quite carefully, but when it comes to the Ten Commandments, Luther breaks the rules. Whereas paraphrase would demand that "You shall not . . ." be paraphrased with "You are to fear and love God so that . . . ," Luther wrote instead, "*We* are to fear and love God. . . ." This small change from "you" to "we" indicates that when it comes to the commandments, all people—listeners *and* the preacher; hearers *and* the teacher—are in the same boat.[12] One can never get past the commandments to live a righteous, holy, or perfect life. Instead, they always destroy before-and-after Christianity and replace it with "the entire life of the faithful is one of penitence."

Think of how this changes evangelism and all of church life! The arrogance of "I have decided to follow Jesus . . . no turning back" gets replaced with "God be merciful to me a sinner." The unbeliever and believer stand in precisely the same place before God: condemned by the law with no claim to make on God's mercy. Even faith cannot divide people into different camps, especially given the poor father's plea in Mark 9 ("I believe; help my unbelief," v. 24)—a favorite verse of Martin Luther and Philip Melanchthon.

The before-and-after myth of Christian existence distorts Scripture and robs it of its good news. Take, for example, the story of the barren fig tree in Luke 13:6–9. The owner wants the tree cut down. In this, his judgment matches all of us, who, although never the owner, are like Ko-Ko, the high executioner for the town of Titipu in Gilbert and Sullivan's *The Mikado*, and have a list of trees we want cut down. Against this judgment, the gardener says, "Give it another year!" Now, at first reading, this story can only sound like a threat to us poor, fruitless trees. And, of course, those with PhDs in "old-creature-hood" (that is, preachers) are only too happy to pile on the guilt and shame: "You've got one year left, and then you're out on your ear!" But the strange thing about this story is that *that* year never comes, cannot come, until the End. Some two thousand years later and people are still telling this story and will continue to tell the story next year and the year after until the good Gardener

---

12. See Timothy J. Wengert, *Martin Luther's Catechisms: Forming the Faith* (Minneapolis: Fortress Press, 2009), 12–13 and 172n21, and the resources cited there.

comes again. Until then and only as this story loses its before-and-after and becomes only "right now," only then do we hear the remarkable good news: "One more year! And another, and another, and another. . . ." This good Gardener never gives up on his fruitless trees.

But finding this surprising good news in the midst of the law's judgment happens only when before-and-after religion itself comes under the law and dies. Otherwise, the law always and only threatens, accuses, and puts to death. Hearing good news in the law's imperatives can occur only when the person receives new life and new ears, so that we hear not simply condemnation for our works but invitation to live by faith alone. Another splendid example of how the death of before-and-after Christianity transforms how we hear Jesus's words comes with the famous "Ask, and it will be given you; search, and you will find; knock, and the door will be opened for you" (Matt 7:7; Luke 11:9). The moralist sucks all the life out of this text by focusing on the imperatives: "Ask . . . search . . . knock"—or else! Then, for example, Job's friends gather around the Syro-Phoenician woman clucking and insisting, "If you only hadn't given up and sought harder and knocked louder. Your daughter's illness is simply a sign of your unbelief, you pagan you!" Under such misuse of the law the remarkable, illogical promise of this text falls silent. After all, what makes this text so remarkable is *not* the command—you don't really have to teach beggars to beg—but the promise. When we ask in this life, often we do not receive; when we look for lost coins, often we do not find them; when we knock, often no one is home. But with God there is always giving, finding, and opening! Who could believe that? What good news!

THE GOSPEL'S USE (BY GOD)

Through the gospel, the Holy Spirit reveals the Savior to the sinner, creates faith in the unbeliever, comforts the terrified, and raises the dead. These expressions indicate how law and gospel work together. In the 1530s, writing in the *Smalcald Articles*, Luther warns that law without gospel is a sure recipe for despair.[13] Without gospel, one could not cry out, "God, be merciful to me, a sinner," because there would only be judgment and wrath—and no mercy. To tell the truth about the human condition (law) without telling the truth about God's merciful heart spells only death.[14] Of course, the gospel itself is a promise, but not just any promise. The conditional promises of the Hebrew Scriptures ("Do this, and you will live") still function as killing letter of the law, although some conditional promises ("Honor you parents . . . so that your days may be long") simply match behavior in this world with the consequences and blessings of this life. Similarly, conditional promises in the New Testament, often connected with reward, are of the same nature. In any case, even conditional promises can still function as promises for blessings and thus do not arise out of human works but out of God's mercy.[15]

But, in fact, the gospel properly speaking contains the unconditional promises of God ("I will be your God"; "I will never leave you or forsake you"; "No one will snatch my sheep out of my hand"). What these promises have in common is a single prepositional phrase: "for you" (or "for me"; "for us"). Luther states this in no uncertain terms when in 1520 he comes to describe good preaching, which is no different from describing good exegesis.

> Preaching, however, ought to serve this goal: that faith in Christ is promoted. Then he is not simply "Christ" but "Christ for you and me," and what we say about him and call him affect us. This faith is born and preserved by preaching why Christ came, what he brought and gave, and what are the needs and the fruit that his reception entail. This kind of preaching occurs where Christian freedom is rightly taught, freedom that we gain from him and that makes us Christians all kings and priests. In him we are lords of all, and we trust that whatever we might do is pleasing and acceptable in God's sight, as we said above.[16]

---

13. SA 3.3.1–9, in BC 312–13.

14. For this language describing the law's work, see James A. Nestingen, "Preaching Repentance," *Lutheran Quarterly* 3 (1989): 249–66.

15. See Ap 4.53–60, in BC 128–30.

16. AL 1:508 (WA 7:58–59).

As soon as we fence in God's promise, it loses its ability to be truly "for you and me," whether we do this by adding "only if you are elect" or "only if you obey the law" or "only if you decide for Jesus." What the old creature cannot stand is precisely the unconditional nature of God's favor and love, because then one's relation to God arises from God and God's mercy and not from us. God's unconditional promise takes that relation completely out of our control.

The "for you/us" of God's Word is all over Scripture. Here is just a sampling. First Peter 2:21: "To this you have been called, because Christ also suffered for you." Titus 2:14: Christ "gave himself for us that he might redeem us." Ephesians 5:2: "Christ loved us and gave himself up for us, a fragrant offering and sacrifice to God." Galatians 3:13: "Christ redeemed us from the curse of the law by becoming a curse for us." Romans 5:8: "But God proves his love for us in that while we were still sinners Christ died for us." In addition, the Pauline and Lukan versions of the Lord's Supper make clear that Christ's body and blood is "given for you" (Luke 22:19–20; 1 Cor 11:24). No wonder the Nicene Creed begins its account of Jesus's incarnation, death, and resurrection with the words "Who for us and for our salvation."

As Luther notes in *Freedom of a Christian*, the "for you" eliminates works and drives us to faith. In 1529, in his explanation of the third article of the creed ("I believe in the Holy Spirit") from the *Small Catechism*, Luther ties the work of the Holy Spirit directly to the gospel, making sure that faith does not simply become another "must" (or, as he said in 1520, a virtue), another work we must somehow manufacture on our own to get on God's good side.

> I believe that by my own understanding or strength I cannot believe in Jesus Christ my Lord or come to him, but instead the Holy Spirit has called me through the gospel, enlightened me with his gifts, made me holy and kept me in the true faith, just as he calls, gathers, enlightens and makes holy the whole Christian church[17] on earth and keeps it with Jesus Christ in the one common, true

---

17. Literally, *Christenheit*. German versions of the creed predating Luther often use this word to translate *ecclesia*.

faith. Daily in this Christian church the Holy Spirit abundantly forgives all sins—mine and those of all believers.[18]

This means that the task of the Christian interpreter is to proclaim (not simply explain) God's unconditional promise from the text, thereby telling the truth about God's mercy for us. Thus the crucial link between what a text says and what it does is the "for you." Then one does not first find out what the biblical text meant before asking what it now means. Instead, the very meaning of the text itself arises from the surprising discovery that it speaks directly to us, to me. Jesus describes this surprise in his parable of the hidden treasure in the field. You just trip over it and find your entire life has changed, so that you have no choice but to sell out, sell all, buy that field. This means that interpretation that does not finally lead to the "for you" simply contains interesting historical or literary facts and serves no real purpose at all. But this also means that interpretation either not based on the text or created simply to manipulate the emotions also is equally unreal.[19]

The gospel with its "for you" creates faith in God. That is its point, its goal. But, as Luther emphasized in *Freedom of a Christian*, faith is not a virtue—something that human beings work on using their own powers—it is rather an experience. It is precisely what happens when the hearer hears the "for you" of the text and gasps, "For me? This gift, this grace, this God, is for me?" The closest experience in daily life to this overwhelming shock of being chosen comes when one person proposes marriage to another. Whether on the Jumbotron of a sports stadium, captured on video for YouTube, or done in a completely intimate setting, the reaction of joy and disbelief combined shows up over and over again. The experience of good news does some-

18. SC, "Creed," 6, in BC 355–56.
19. AL 1:508 (WA 7:58). "I believe that it has become clear that it is not sufficient or even Christian if, as those who are the very best preachers today do, we only preach Christ's works, life and words just as a kind of story or as historical exploits (which would be enough to know in providing an example of how to conduct our lives). Much worse is when there is complete silence about Christ, and human laws and the decrees of the fathers are taught instead of Christ. Moreover, some even preach Christ and recite stories about him for this purpose: to play on human emotions either to arouse sympathy for him or to incite anger against the Jews. This kind of thing is simply childish and over-emotional nonsense."

thing to the hearer. For this reason, Luther concluded his discussion of preaching in *Freedom of a Christian* with these words:

> What person's heart upon hearing these things would not rejoice from its very core and upon accepting such consolation would not melt in love with Christ—something completely unattainable with laws and works? Who could possibly harm or frighten such a heart? If awareness of sin or dread of death overwhelms it, it is ready to hope in the Lord. It neither fears hearing about these evils nor is moved by them, until finally it despises its enemies. For it believes that Christ's righteousness is its own and that its sin is now not its own but Christ's. More than that, the presence of Christ's righteousness swallows up every sin. As noted above, this is a necessary consequence of faith in Christ. So the heart learns with the Apostle to scoff at death and sin and to say: "Where, O death, is your victory? Where, O death, is your sting? The sting of death is sin, and the power of sin is the law. But thanks be to God, who gives us the victory through our Lord Jesus Christ." For death is swallowed up in victory—not only Christ's but ours—because through faith it becomes our victory and is in us and we are conquerors.[20]

At this point, someone may object that Luther was talking about preaching, which is hardly the same as discussing biblical interpretation. If, however, as Gerhard Forde once demonstrated, "theology is for proclamation," then the same may be said of biblical exegesis.[21] If it does not lead to proclamation, to the "for you" of the text, then it is merely historical exploits (Latin: *res gestae*) and has next to nothing to do with the *meaning* of the text itself, because it glibly eliminates the author and original hearer's intention and the intention of the church that has preserved this writing as Word of God. Moreover, by ignoring the "for you," biblical interpreters leave the text open to the "antitext" of legalism and emotionalism.

For example, Luther knew full well that during Holy Week preaching on Jesus's passion led to attacks on the Jews. Despite his own despicable record of anti-Jewish writings, Luther regularly rejected preaching that gave people an excuse to persecute

---

20. AL 1:509 (WA 7:59).
21. Gerhard Forde, *Theology Is for Proclamation* (Minneapolis: Fortress Press, 1990).

Jews.[22] This kind of childish, overemotional manipulation makes clear that one cannot simply recite the passion story with its "His blood be upon us" (Matt 27:25) and "We have no king but Caesar" (John 19:15 KJV) and all the rest without turning the text away from the original speakers and toward the hearers today. Thus Luther regularly insists that he and his hearers and their sins have crucified Christ—a sentiment expressed a century later by the German hymn writer: "'Twas I, Lord Jesus, I it was denied Thee; I crucified Thee."

THE LAW'S CIVIL USE AND GOD'S TWO HANDS

Even though the "civil use" of the law is often labeled the "first use," it turns out that the Wittenberg Reformers first began to work out this category after they had already been using "law and gospel" for several years. Although it is not hard to find passages in Luther's early works that foreshadow this "first use," it began to take shape while Luther was at the Wartburg, when Melanchthon sent him a letter (now lost) asking about the arts faculty.[23] Was it really necessary for Christians to concern themselves with such mundane things as the arts, or should they simply stick with the gospel? Luther insisted to his younger colleague that there was indeed a place for such teaching. On the basis of this advice, Melanchthon began to change his approach to life in this world, adding several paragraphs to the 1522 second printing of his 1521 *Loci communes* on the subject. In subsequent writings, too, he began to insist that the law had a positive use in this world: restraining evil and keeping order.

Luther, too, soon began to write about God's good order and the battle against evil in this world. This culminated in his important (but often misunderstood) statements about God's two realms (kingdoms) or governments, which might better be designated "God's Two Hands."[24] To be sure, through "law and

22. See, for two examples, AL 1:169 and 508 (WA 2:136 and 7:58).

23. Timothy J. Wengert, "Philip Melanchthon and a Christian *Politics*," *Lutheran Quarterly* 17 (2003): 29–62, esp. 40–44.

24. With the left hand, God is maintaining order and restraining evil in this world; with the right, God announces the world to come, when all evil will be destroyed. This topic is among the most widely debated in Luther scholarship today. See the

gospel" God's right hand is ushering *in the new world* as sheer, merciful promise. But already from creation, with the left hand God has been establishing good order *in this world*, including both creation itself and the household (and, by extension, the household's helpers—government, school, and the like). In the face of human rebellion, God's good order also functions to restrain evil so that human beings can live peaceable lives and believers (the sheep of God's pasture) can find protection against the ungodly. Melanchthon's 1527 commentary on Colossians names these two offices or functions of the law. While Luther does not often use systematic categories for such matters, in the *Smalcald Articles*, published in 1538, he writes this description:

> Concerning the Law. Here we maintain that the law was given by God, in the first place, to curb sin by means of the threat and terror of punishment and also by means of the promise and offer of grace and favor. All of this failed because of the evil that sin worked in humankind. Some, who are enemies of the law because it prohibits what they want to do and commands what they do not want to do, became worse because of it. On account of this, in so far as they are not restrained by punishment, they act against the law even more than before. These are the coarse, evil people who do evil whenever they have an opportunity. Others become blind and presumptuous, imagining that they can and do keep the law by their own powers (as has just been said above about the scholastic theologians). This attitude produces hypocrites and false saints.
>
> The foremost office or power of the law is that it reveals inherited sin and its fruits. It shows human beings into what utter depths their nature has fallen and how completely corrupt it is. The law must say to them that they neither have nor respect any god or that they worship foreign gods. This is something that they would not have believed before without the law. Thus they are terrified, humbled, despondent, and despairing. They anxiously desire help but do not know where to find it; they start to become enemies of God, to murmur, etc. This is what is meant by Romans [4:15]:

summary of Luther's ethical teaching in Robert Kolb, *Martin Luther: Confessor of the Faith* (New York: Oxford University Press, 2009), 172–96; and William J. Wright, *Martin Luther's Understanding of God's Two Kingdoms: A Response to the Challenge of Skepticism* (Grand Rapids: Baker Academic, 2010).

"The law brings wrath," and Romans 5[:20] "Sin becomes greater through the law."[25]

What is missing from this description of the first use is the more positive notion of God's ordering of creation.[26] This Luther dealt with in other venues, especially when describing the positive aspects of the household and government. Thus his explanation of the fourth commandment in the *Large Catechism* set out what God is actually doing through this and the following commandments.

> God has given this walk of life, fatherhood and motherhood, a special position of honor, higher than that of any other walk of life under it. Not only has he commanded us to love parents but to honor them. In regard to brothers, sisters, and neighbors in general he commands nothing higher than that we love them. But he distinguishes father and mother above all other persons on earth, and places them next to himself. For it is a much higher thing to honor than to love. Honor includes not only love, but also deference, humility, and modesty directed (so to speak) toward a majesty concealed within them. . . . In the second place, notice what a great, good, and holy work is here assigned to children. Unfortunately, it is entirely despised and brushed aside, and no one recognizes it as God's command or as a holy, divine word and teaching.[27]

Luther then introduced his standard criticism of monasticism for breaking familial ties and for boasting of a higher spirituality than life under the fourth commandment. He also emphasized that from parents all other earthly powers derive their authority, whether heads of households (often employers), teachers, pastors, or leaders in government. Yet the good work commanded in this commandment does not affect one's standing before God.

---

25. SA 3.2.1–5, in BC 311–12.

26. The nineteenth-century Lutheran ethicist Gottlieb Christoph Adolf von Harleß first coined the term "orders of creation" and used it to emphasize that these orders were not eternally fixed but subject to change. Not long thereafter, however, theologians began to use them in the opposite sense, and some German theologians then added the nation as a fourth order (beyond household, government, and church). See Timothy J. Wengert, *Reading the Bible with Martin Luther* (Grand Rapids: Baker Academic, 2013), 69–70.

27. LC, Ten Commandments, 105–6, 112, in BC 400–401.

Nowhere did Luther make this clearer than in his statements about servants of the household.

> If this could be impressed on the poor people, a servant girl would dance for joy and praise and thank God; and with her careful work, for which she receives sustenance and wages, she would obtain a treasure such as those who are regarded as the greatest saints do not have. Is it not a tremendous honor to know this and to say, "If you do your daily household chores, that is better than the holiness and austere life of all the monks"? Moreover, you have the promise that whatever you do will prosper and fare well. How could you be more blessed or lead a holier life, as far as works are concerned? In God's sight it is actually faith that makes a person holy; it alone serves God, while our works serve people.[28]

"In God's sight . . . faith," Luther stated, thus distinguishing the work of "[law and] gospel," which creates faith through God's mercy in Christ, and life in this world and its works. Thus his criticism of monasticism derives from his general criticism of confusing human works with God's grace and imagining that the former merits the latter. Instead, through the fourth commandment the Creator has fashioned the office of parent (and child) for life in this world. In this and the succeeding commandments, we find God's will for all humanity revealed.

In this way, Luther's expositions of the fourth through eighth commandments function as his social ethics. In the fourth commandment, in addition to praising the offices of parent, householder (i.e., employer), and ruler, he also restricts their authority by the first three commandments and by God's intention that those in authority view children, workers, and subjects not as objects for exploitation but as gifts entrusted to them by God. The fifth through eighth commandments further show the particulars of life together: caring for the poor, loving one's spouse, not exploiting the poor, and protecting the neighbor's reputation. Rather than concoct some sort of special "Christian" ethic, Luther insists on the down-to-earth alternative, under which all human beings must live: "Love your neighbor as yourself."

Interpreting biblical texts in the light of this first use has proved to be more complicated in our day than in Luther's.

28. LC, Ten Commandments, 145–47, in BC 406.

Sometimes, for example, preaching obedience to government has become a cover for supporting tyranny and the destruction of not only good government but also the gospel itself. Yet Luther's comments on the fourth commandment in the *Large Catechism* insisted that the first three commandments are over the fourth. (In other situations, the Wittenberg Reformers cited Acts 5:29.)[29] He also underscored that, despite the fact that the fourth commandment places *no* conditions on such obedience, other passages of Scripture make clear that parents and their governmental "helpers" are not to abuse family members or subjects.[30]

Misuse of the first use of the law can promote hyper-obedience and can also confuse law and gospel when preachers and teachers imagine that the law, especially the law of Christ, is part of the gospel. This confusion, rampant among both liberal and conservative Christians in the United States, results in, for example, a quest for a "Christian America," where the maintenance or enactment of certain laws will supposedly ensure God's blessing (and failure, God's curse). Then the verse "Blessed is the nation whose God is the Lord" becomes a cover for all kinds of Christian legalism, and a text aimed at God's Israel suddenly becomes a pretext for efforts to improve American morals.[31] But this confusion is not just a problem among conservatives. Liberal Protestants, too, have only too happily equated "peace and justice" with the gospel, when such appeals are always strictly "law." As soon as "forgiveness, life, and salvation" get replaced by "justice, peace, and inclusivity" (or any other triumvirate), then hearers and readers return home with an *agenda*, "things that must be done," and God's mercy—from which all truly good works come—is drowned in a sea of guilt and shame or hyperactive "works of love." The very spontaneity that marks Christian life falls again under servility to the law, and, to misquote John 15, "we are no longer friends but slaves."

29. CA 16.6–7, in BC 50.

30. LC, Ten Commandments, 167–73, in BC 409–10.

31. See the still classic Robert T. Handy, *A Christian America: Protestant Hopes and Historical Realities* (New York: Oxford University Press, 1971).

WHAT ABOUT A THIRD USE OF THE LAW?

Inevitably, whenever Lutherans talk about law and gospel, someone asks about a third use of the law, that is, about a separate use of the law reserved as a special guide for Christians. Although most Luther scholars now insist that Luther did not develop such a category in his thought, a recent publication claims to refute such supposed animosity toward the law implied in those scholars' writings.[32] People imagine that those who deny Luther employed a third use of the law make him and his followers into antinomians, willing to let just about anything go. In order to understand where such a third use arose, it is important to trace the specific origin of the terminology and why, for Philip Melanchthon and his adherents (and thus for later Lutherans), this category was deemed to be so useful.

In 1997 and 1998 this author published two studies of Philip Melanchthon's first commentary on Colossians, initially published in 1527 and revised twice (in 1528 and 1534).[33] Because next to no one had bothered to read the 1534 commentary, it came as quite a surprise to many scholars that in that commentary, for the first time ever, Melanchthon defined three uses of the law: a civil use (to restrain evil and provide order in this world), a theological use (to reveal sin and drive to Christ), and a catechetical use for Christians (one that revealed God's will for the believer). A year later, Melanchthon expounded on this third use in his second edition of the *Loci communes theologici*, the main textbook for students of Wittenberg's theology. And a year after that, John Calvin included a third use of the law in the first edition of the *Institutes*, probably borrowing from Melanchthon's Colossians commentary.

32. Edward A. Engelbrecht, *Friends of the Law: Luther's Use of the Law for the Christian Life* (St. Louis: Concordia, 2011), 7–8. See my review in *International Journal of Systematic Theology* 17 (2015): 481–84.

33. Timothy J. Wengert, *Human Freedom, Christian Righteousness: Philip Melanchthon's Exegetical Dispute with Erasmus of Rotterdam* (New York: Oxford University Press, 1998); and Wengert, *Law and Gospel: Philip Melanchthon's Debate with John Agricola of Eisleben over "Poenitentia"* (Grand Rapids: Baker, 1997), for this paragraph, esp. 177–210.

One major difference always distinguished a Lutheran under-standing of a "third use" from that of Calvin and his supporters. Calvin insisted that this third use, as a guide for Christian living, was the law's central function.[34] Melanchthon and Luther always insisted that the chief function of the law was to drive humanity to Christ, that is, its second, theological function. Moreover, Calvin also insisted that such Christian laws were unique to Christians and thus placed them in a relationship to God dif-ferent from that of unbelievers. Melanchthon and Luther were far more skeptical that Christians possessed some special revela-tion of the law.[35] For them, the gospel was the one thing that went beyond reason and was unique to Christians. New Testa-ment believers had no special set of laws or principles by which to govern their lives. Already the Ten Commandments summa-rized the law completely, so that even the command in John 13 ("Love one another") arose out of the Decalogue. Indeed, the most accurate definition of the *Lutheran* third use of the law is simply the first and second use of the law applied to the believer. This certainly is the point in the Formula of Concord, written by Luther's and Melanchthon's students in 1576.[36]

But why did Melanchthon introduce a third use precisely in 1534? The answer comes from the immediate context. In 1534, Melanchthon was involved in discussions with some of Wit-tenberg's more moderate Catholic opponents in Leipzig. These theologians insisted that, based on John 13 and Jesus's "new commandment," the law was part of the gospel. Melanchthon responded by insisting that the command to "love one another," even though addressed to Jesus's disciples, was still law, and he proposed that in addition to the law functioning to maintain order in the world and reveal sin, there was a third use, directed

---

34. See John Calvin, *Institutes of the Christian Religion*, ed. John T. McNeill, trans. Ford Lewis Battles (Philadelphia: Westminster, 1960), 2.7.12–13 (1:360–61).

35. One way to measure the secondary importance of the third use of the law comes from Melanchthon himself. Although the text of the Colossians commentary from 1534 talked of three uses, the printer neglected to change the marginal note, which still talked of only two uses. Moreover, when Melanchthon revised his com-mentary on Romans in 1540, he still defined only two uses of the law.

36. See *Formula of Concord*, Solid Declaration, art. 6, in BC 587–91; and Timothy J. Wengert, *A Formula for Parish Practice: Using the Formula of Concord in the Parish* (Grand Rapids: Eerdmans, 2006), 90–102.

toward Christians. Nevertheless, it was still law and not to be confused with the gospel of God's mercy and forgiveness in Christ. At the same time, Melanchthon was still very skeptical of Johann Agricola, whom he had attacked already in the 1527 edition of the Colossians commentary as part of a prelude to the Antinomian Controversy of the late 1530s. Agricola, rector of Eisleben's Latin school, insisted that the law was not central to theology and, as his later supporters put it, belonged only in city hall and not the pulpit. Against this position, Melanchthon (like Luther) argued that because of the old creature in believers, the law was needed to restrain evil and reveal sin. It also helped clarify God's loving will for humanity and creation, so that the Christian need not be uncertain about which good works pleased God. The passages in the 1527 and 1528 Colossians commentaries that had initially attacked Agricola were the places where Melanchthon added a third use of the law in 1534.

As Luther made clear in his subsequent attack on Agricola's antinomianism, the believer could not simply wish the law out of existence, since it continues to attack the sinner in each of us. Such a dismissal was rather like "putting on a play in an empty theater," he wrote. Indeed, the old creature is always at war against the law, as Luke says in introducing the parable of the good Samaritan: "But he, wishing to justify himself. . . ." If the old creature can simply reduce the number of neighbors to whom a person is responsible, then perhaps he or she can fulfill the law. This, along with hundreds of other obfuscations, finally does not work. The neighbor with his or her needs still lies on the side of the road, beaten and bruised, demanding by these very wounds our help. As Karl Barth is reputed to have said, "True, the old creature is drowned in baptism, but it is a good underwater swimmer." Only the law can catch the culprit and drag it back under the water—daily. That is, there is no "before-and-after" in the Christian life, only the *simul* of baptism's drowning and rising.

So, in light of these two countervailing forces—one nomian and one antinomian—Melanchthon insisted that faith did not destroy the law, precisely *because* believers are at the same time justified and sinner. Once again, Luther's initial challenge to late-medieval before-and-after Christianity comes to expression in the third use of the law. There are, however, some awkward sides to this "use" of the law, precisely because the "user" seems to shift somewhat from God (who keeps order and puts to death) to the believer, who now "uses" the law as a guide. Here, the weaker one's view of the Holy Spirit, the more likely the individual takes center stage (thereby breaking the first commandment). It would be better to say that the Holy Spirit continues to use the law, à la John 16:8, to condemn sin and raise up a new person of faith daily.

Even the revelation of God's heart at the center of the commandments comes as a result of faith, which offers a completely new perspective on God's law, turning it from unfulfillable demand for the old creature to loving invitation for the new. Martin Luther touched on this transformation in the one paragraph on prayer that he added to the second printing of the *Large Catechism* in 1529. There he depicted the old creature always fleeing from God, so that God gives the commandment to pray (which Luther derived from the second commandment) as a way of overcoming its conviction that God will not listen to sinners.

> Indeed, the human heart is by nature so desperately wicked that it always flees from God, thinking that he neither wants nor cares for our prayers because we are sinners and have merited nothing but wrath. . . . By this [second] commandment [God] makes it clear that he will not cast us out or drive us away, even though we are sinners; he wishes rather to draw us to himself so that we may humble ourselves before him, lament our misery and plight, and pray for grace and help.[37]

Commands and invitations, despite their grammatical similarities, are as different as night and day. A convict, told to call his or her parole officer every week, differs completely from a lover who receives an invitation, attached to a note containing the writer's unlisted phone number, saying "Call me!" In the former case, it is a burden and a threat, forcing a person to do what they may very well not want to do at all. In the latter case, it is an

---

37. LC, Lord's Prayer, 10–11, in BC 441–42.

exciting, love-creating, and sustaining word. "You mean, you want me to call you? You like me; you really like me!"[38]

In the section on the third use of the law in the Formula of Concord, the second generation of Lutheran Reformers, led in this case by Andreas Musculus of Brandenburg, made the same distinction.

> However, when people are born again through the Spirit of God and set free from the law (that is, liberated from its driving powers and driven by the Spirit of Christ), they live according to the unchanging will of God, as comprehended in the law, and do everything, in so far as they are reborn, from a free and merry spirit. Works of this kind are not, properly speaking, works of the law but works and fruits of the Spirit, or, as Paul calls them, "the law of the mind" and "the law of Christ." For such people are "no longer under law but under grace," as Saint Paul says in Romans 8 [7:23; 6:14]. However, since believers in this world are not perfectly renewed—the old creature clings to them down to the grave—the battle between spirit and flesh continues in them. Therefore, they indeed desire to perform the law of God according to their inner person, but the law in their members struggles against the law of their mind [Rom 7:23]. To this extent they are never without the law, and at the same time they are not under the law but in the law; they live and walk in the law of the Lord and yet do nothing because of the compulsion of the law. As far as the old creature, which still clings to them, is concerned, it must be driven not only by the law but also by tribulations because it does everything against its own will, under compulsion, no less than the godless are driven by the threats of the law and are thus kept obedient (1 Cor. 9[:27], Rom. 7[:18,19]).[39]

Striking here is the reference to Romans 7, that premier text in Scripture discussing the *simul iustus et peccator*. This demonstrates that Lutheran hermeneutics are intimately bound to

---

38. Echoing the reaction of Sally Field upon receiving an Oscar: "I can't deny the fact that you like me; right now you like me."

39. Solid Declaration, 6.17–19, in BC 590. This also sets aside the charge that, as a result of their narrow view of the law as always accusing, Lutheran exegetes misread Paul and reject the Torah. Not only is the Torah filled with promises (culminating in the phrase repeated constantly in Leviticus, "I am your God"), but also its laws reveal God's heart: for Israel especially but, when viewed in Abraham's faith, for all of his descendants.

Lutheran anthropology.[40] This is particularly true of the third use of the law, where John Calvin (along with many who follow him—Reformed and Lutheran theologians alike) makes the third use of the law central and replaces the Lutheran rejection of before-and-after Christianity with an understanding of salvation history that moves the elect inexorably from sin to faith. For Lutherans, the law always accuses the old creature and, at the same time (*simul*), invites the forgiven believer into God's heart, where it eagerly serves God "with a free and merry spirit." Thus, for those who insist on preaching the law's third use (if that is even possible), one measure of success would be whether the hearers walk out of church either whistling (a sure sign of a free and merry spirit) or simply burdened.

LAW AND GOSPEL FOR TODAY

The distinction between law and gospel—defined now as a distinction not between imperatives and indicatives (commands and promises) but between the two chief effects of hearing God's Word (death and resurrection or terror and comfort)—puts the lie to much of what passes as legitimate biblical exegesis today. When the meaning of a text and its effect are completely separated, the interpreter has no choice but to moralize. For example, a sermon on "God is love" becomes an exhortation to the hearers to love others. This turns the text upside down. Then one is left with the impression that if I love God, then God will love me. Then the "free and merry spirit" of faith (that proclaims "because God loves me, therefore I am free to love others") is crushed under the burden of conditional Christianity and the grace of the believing sinner's simultaneous life is lost. Then it does not really matter what kind of conditions one heaps on the hapless listener, the results are the same: either the pride of the Pharisee in Luke 18 ("I thank you, God, that I am not like that sinner over there") or the despair of unbelief ("God can never love me").

This misapprehension is especially true of America's conservative and liberal Christians, all of whom agree that the "real" Christian message is a set of rules to live by—something that

40. Kolb, *Martin Luther*, 105–9.

should never be confused with the gospel and actually belongs on God's left hand, in this world, with the law's civil, first use. As long as most non-Christians, when asked about the nature of Christianity, respond by pointing to doctrines, laws, or future speculation (the three spiritual meanings of the Quadriga), then the gospel, the unconditional good news of God in Christ reconciling the world to himself, remains under a bench, gathering dust. But despite the old creature's best intentions, God is in charge of God's word and we are not. God will have the last, gracious word: a word filled with forgiveness, life, and salvation; a word that frees the forgiven sinner to live life in this world awaiting God's mercy in Christ each day.

4.

Famous Last Words

Beginning in the Middle Ages in the West, Holy Week was often a special time for preaching, with priests and bishops concentrating remarks on the passion of Christ. As we have seen, Luther even criticized some of these sermons for inciting attacks on the Jews. Indeed, we know that especially in the late Middle Ages Holy Week sermons instigated pogroms against Jewish inhabitants of Western Europe. Luther, by insisting that the whole human race including his hearers were guilty of Christ's death, undermined this traditional preaching. Nevertheless, he continued preaching during Holy Week on Christ's passion, in later years using the harmonization of the passion story published by Wittenberg's chief pastor, Johannes Bugenhagen.[1]

At least in the United States, Lutherans and others in the twentieth century came to preach on the same harmonization during Wednesdays in Lent leading up to Holy Week. But they, along with other Protestants, also developed the tradition, borrowed from a seventeenth-century (Latin American?) Roman Catholic tradition designed to educate people about Christ's passion, of Good Friday preaching on the seven last words of Jesus: one shared in Matthew and Mark, three each in Luke and John. Starting in 2006, as a member of St. Matthew Lutheran Church,

---

1. See Johannes Bugenhagen, *Conciliata ex Evangelistis historia passi Christi & glorificati, cum annotationibus,* in *Annotationes . . . iam emissae in Deuteronomium, in Samuelem prophetam, id est, duos libros Regum* (Basel: Petri, 1524).

Moorestown, New Jersey, I would be asked by the pastor—my wife, Ingrid Wengert—to preach on one of the seven last words at a worship service organized and held at the local Episcopal church. These sermons, along with a sermon on Christ the King Sunday, contain reflections on five of the seven words, and I offer them below. To these I have added two other meditations composed for this book.

To be sure, the Revised Common Lectionary's guidelines—to read one of the Synoptic Gospels' Passion story on Palm (Passion) Sunday and John's account on Good Friday—are far more respectful of the individual Gospels. I believe that Christians best view the four Gospels separately from one another, using the resources within each Gospel to interpret the entire passion story in context. This avoids the kind of overharmonization that sometimes obscures an author's individual approach to telling the story. For example, the clear change in John's Gospel of the very date of the crucifixion from Passover to the day before Passover, which has posed a conundrum for ancient and modern exegetes, may best be appropriated by leaving aside the historical question of harmonizing the accounts and instead assuming that John's point has far more to do with one of the chief themes in his Gospel ("Behold the Lamb of God") than with anything else—especially since his dating matches the time Passover lambs were slaughtered. Worry over harmonizing the Gospels (or even calling one version correct and the other in error or explaining that one is based on a different way to calculate the Passover) simply misses John's main point—underscored by his reference to Exodus 12. (In his 1523 commentary on John, Melanchthon also provided an extensive allegory of the Passover as a way of emphasizing its role in John's Gospel.)

That these are sermons and not "pure" exegesis should not alarm the reader, since this well matches the central hermeneutic emanating from Wittenberg: that definition and effect constitute the true meaning of the text. Exegesis *is* for proclamation, and these sermons are intended to give the reader some assistance in both at the same time. Preceding these sermons is Luther's meditation on Christ's passion from 1519.

MARTIN LUTHER ON THE PASSION OF CHRIST

In 1519, probably during Holy Week, Luther preached on Christ's passion, as was expected in his day. His sermon, clearly revised for publication, was one of his most popular and important publications. It not only enjoyed many reprints but also became included in his *Church Postil*, where it continued to influence preachers and teachers into the twenty-first century. It shows Luther's strong debt to his "mystical" rooting among the Augustinian friars and to late-medieval piety. But it also includes criticisms of that very religiosity, especially regarding Holy Week preaching and the Lord's Supper. The following translation, without the accompanying notes and introduction, comes from the *Annotated Luther*.[2]

> 1. Some people meditate on Christ's passion by venting their anger on the Jews, singing and ranting about wretched Judas, which satisfies them, just as they are in the habit of complaining about other people, of condemning and reproaching their adversaries. That might well be a meditation on the wickedness of Judas and the Jews, but not on the sufferings of Christ.
>
> 2. Some point to the manifold benefits and fruits that grow from contemplating Christ's passion. There is a saying ascribed to St. Albert about this, that it is more beneficial to ponder Christ's passion just once than to fast a whole year or to pray a psalm daily, etc. These people follow this saying blindly and therefore do not reap the fruit of Christ's passion, for in so doing they are seeking their own advantage. They carry pictures and booklets, letters and crosses on their person. Some go so far afield as to imagine that they thus protect themselves against water and sword, fire, and all sorts of perils. Christ's suffering is used to work in them a lack of suffering, contrary to Christ's being and nature.
>
> 3. Some feel pity for Christ, lamenting and bewailing his innocence. They are like the women who followed Christ from Jerusalem and were upbraided by Christ that it would be better to weep for themselves and their children [Luke 23:27–28]. They are the kind of people who go far afield in their meditation on

2. AL 1:167–79. For a broader discussion of Luther's early pastoral writings, see Anna Marie Johnson, *Beyond Indulgences: Luther's Reform of Late Medieval Piety, 1518–1520* (Kirksville, MO: Truman State University Press, 2017), esp. for this tract, 116–20.

the passion, making much of Christ's farewell from Bethany [John 12:1–18] and of the Virgin Mary's anguish [John 19:25–27] but never progressing beyond that, which is why so many hours are devoted to the contemplation of Christ's passion. Only God knows whether the purpose is for sleeping or for staying awake.

This group also includes those who have learned what rich fruits the holy mass offers. In their simplemindedness they think it enough just to hear mass. In support of this, several teachers are cited for us who hold that the mass is *opere operati, non opere operantis*, that it is effective in itself without our merit and worthiness, as if this were all that is needed. Yet the mass was not instituted for its own worthiness but to make us worthy and to bring us to meditate on the Christ's passion. Where that is not done, we turn the mass into a physical and unfruitful act, even though the mass is good in and of itself. But of what help is it to you that God is God, if God is not God for you? Of what benefit is it that eating and drinking are good and healthy if they are not healthy for you? And it is to be feared that many masses will not improve matters as long as we do not seek the right fruit in it.

4. They contemplate Christ's passion properly who look at it with a terrified heart and a despairing conscience. This terror must be felt as you witness the stern wrath and the unchanging seriousness with which God looks upon sin and sinners, so much so that God did not want to release sinners to his only beloved Son unless he did such heavy penance for them. As God says in Isaiah 53[:8], "For the sins of my people I have struck him." If the dearest child is punished in this way, what will sinners encounter? An inexpressible and unbearable matter of deadly seriousness must be present for such a great and infinite person to defy it and to suffer and die for it. And if you seriously consider that it is God's very own Son, the eternal wisdom of the Father, who suffers, you will truly be terrified, and the more you consider this the deeper the terror.

5. You must impress this deeply in your mind and not doubt that you are the one who makes Christ suffer in this way, for your sins have certainly caused this. In Acts 2[:36–37] St. Peter frightened the Jews like a peal of thunder when he said to all of them, "You crucified him." Consequently, on that same day three thousand came to the apostles, terrified and shaking, and asked, "O dear brothers, what should we do now?" Therefore, when you see the nails piercing Christ's hands, you can be certain that it is your work. When you behold his crown of thorns, you may rest assured that these are your evil thoughts, and so on.

6. For every nail that pierces Christ, more than one hundred thousand should in justice pierce you; yes, they should pierce you forever and more painfully! When Christ is tortured by nails penetrating his hands and feet, you should eternally suffer the pain they inflict and the pain of even crueler nails, which will in truth happen to those who allow Christ's passion to be lost on them, because this stern mirror, Christ, will not lie or be trifled with, and whatever it points out must be completely overwhelming.

7. St. Bernard drew out from this such terror that he said, "I thought I was secure; I was not aware of the eternal sentence that had been passed on me in heaven until I saw that God's only Son had compassion upon me and offered to bear this judgment for me. Alas, if the situation is that serious, I should not make light of it or feel secure." We read that Christ commanded the women not to weep for him but for themselves and their children [Luke 23:28]. And he adds the reason for this, saying [Luke 23:31], "For if they do this to the green wood, what will happen when it is dry?" It is as if he had said: "From my torture learn what you deserve and what should happen to you." Here the saying applies that the small dog is whipped to frighten the big dog. Thus the prophet said that "on his account all the tribes of the earth will wail for themselves"; the prophet does not say that they will wail for him, but that they will wail for themselves because of him. In like manner the people of whom we heard in Acts 2[:36–37] were so terrified that they said to the apostles, "O brothers, what should we do?" This is also the song of the church: "I will ponder this diligently and, as a result, my soul will languish within me."

8. On this point, we should truly exercise ourselves, for the main benefit of Christ's passion is that individuals recognize their own true selves and be terrified and crushed by what they see. And when they do not come to this point, they do not yet derive any benefit from Christ's passion. The real and true work of Christ's passion is to conform individuals to Christ, so that as Christ was miserably tormented in body and soul by our sins we, following him, may be tormented by our sins in our conscience. This does not call for many words but for profound reflection and a great attention to sins. Consider this illustration: a criminal is sentenced to death for the murder of the child of a prince or a king. In the meantime you go your carefree way, singing and playing, until you are cruelly arrested and convicted of having incited the murderer. Now the whole world closes in upon you, especially since your conscience also deserts you. You should be terrified even more when you meditate on Christ's passion. For the evildoers, the

Jews, whom God has judged and driven out, were only the servants of your sin; you are actually the one who, as we said, by your sin executed and crucified God's Son.

9. The one who is so hardhearted and callous as to be neither frightened by Christ's passion nor led to a knowledge of self, has reason to fear. There is no avoiding being conformed to Christ's image and suffering, whether in this life or in hell. At the very least, you will sink into this terror at the hour of death and in purgatory and will tremble and quake and feel all that Christ suffered on the cross. Since it is horrible to lie waiting on your deathbed, you should pray God to soften your heart and let you ponder Christ's passion in fruitful ways. For unless God buries it in our hearts, it is impossible for us, on our own, to meditate thoroughly on Christ's passion. Neither this meditation nor any other teaching is given to you so that you might jump on it completely on your own in order to master it. Rather, first you should seek and desire God's grace so that you master it not by your own power but by God's grace. That is why the people we referred to above fail to deal correctly with Christ's passion. They do not call upon God's help but look to their own ability to invent their own means of accomplishing this [meditation]. They deal with the matter in a completely human and unfruitful way.

10. We say without hesitation that those who contemplate God's sufferings for a day, an hour, yes, only a quarter of an hour, do better than to fast a whole year, pray a psalm daily, yes, better than to hear a hundred masses. This meditation transforms a person's being and, almost like baptism, gives a new birth. Here the passion of Christ performs its natural and noble work, executing the old Adam and expelling all joy, delight, and confidence that a person could find in other creatures, even as Christ was forsaken by all, even by God.

11. Since this work does not rest with us, it happens that we will sometimes pray for it, and yet not attain it at once. Nevertheless we should neither despair nor desist. At times this happens because we do not pray for it as God indicates and wishes it, for it must be left free and unfettered. Then a person becomes sad in conscience and grumbles inwardly about the evil in life. It may well be that, even when such a one does not think about Christ's passion, it is working this [death] within, just as these others, who do think of Christ's passion all the time, do not attain self-knowledge through it. For the former [persons] the passion of Christ is hidden and genuine, while for the latter it is only an outer shell and misleading. In this way God often reverses matters, so that those who do

not meditate on Christ's passion do meditate on it, and those who do not hear mass do hear it, and those who hear it do not hear it.

12. Until now we have sojourned in Holy Week and rightly celebrated Good Friday. Now we come to the resurrection of Christ, to the day of Easter. After a person becomes aware of sin and terrified at heart, that one must watch that sin does not remain in the conscience, for this would certainly lead to nothing but doubt. Instead, as soon as sins have flowed from [meditating on] Christ and are recognized, so they must be shaken back on him and the conscience emptied of them. Therefore, watch out that you do not do as those perverse people who gnaw at and devour their hearts with their sins and, running to and fro, strive to get rid of their sins through good works or [penitential acts of] satisfaction, or to work their way out of this by means of indulgences. Unfortunately such false confidence in penance and pilgrimages is widespread.

13. You throw your sins off of yourself and onto Christ when you firmly believe that his wounds and sufferings are your sins, that he carries and pays for them, as we read in Isa. 53[:6], "The Lord has laid on him the iniquity of us all." And St. Peter says [1 Pet 2:24], "He himself bore our sins in his body on the cross." St. Paul says [2 Cor 5:21], "For our sake God made him to be sin who knew no sin, so that in him we might become the righteousness of God." You must completely rely on these and similar verses—the more your conscience tortures you, the more you must rely on them. If you do not do that, but presume to still your conscience with your contrition and satisfaction, you will never come to peace and in the end will only doubt. For if we allow sin to remain in our conscience and try to deal with it there, or if we look at sin in our heart, it will be much too strong for us and will live on forever. But if we see that it rests on Christ and is overcome by his resurrection, and then boldly believe this, then sin is dead and nullified. For sin cannot remain on Christ, since it is swallowed up by his resurrection, and so now you see no wounds or no pain in him, that is, no sign of sin. As St. Paul declares [Rom 4:25], "Christ was handed over to death for our trespasses and was raised for our justification," that is, in his suffering Christ reveals our sin and thereby executes it, but through his resurrection Christ makes us righteous and free of all sin, when we believe this.

14. If, as was said before, you cannot believe, you should ask God for faith. But this too rests entirely in the hands of God who gives faith sometimes openly, sometimes in secret, as was said earlier about suffering. If you wish to rouse yourself to faith, first of all, you should no longer contemplate the suffering of Christ (for this

has already done its work and terrified you). Instead, pass through that and see Christ's friendly heart and how full of love it is towards you that it impels him to carry with heaviness your conscience and your sin. Then your heart will be sweet towards him, and the confidence of faith will be strengthened. Now go further and rise through Christ's heart to God's heart, and you will see that Christ would not have shown this love for you if God, to whom Christ with his love for you is obedient, did not want to hold [you] in eternal love. There you will find the divine, good, fatherly heart, and, as Christ says [cf. John 14:6], you will be drawn to the Father through him. Then you will understand the words of Christ [John 3:16], "For God so loved the world that he gave his only Son. . . ." That is, we know God properly when we grasp God not in God's power or wisdom (which is terrifying), but in God's kindness and love. Then faith and confidence are able to exist, and then a person is truly born anew in God.

15. When your heart has thus become firm in Christ, and you have become an enemy of sin from love and not the fear of suffering, then from that day on Christ's passion should become an example for your entire life, and you will now see his passion differently. Until now we regarded it as a sacrament that is active in us while we are passive, but now we find that we too must be active, namely, in the following ways:

If pain or sickness afflicts you, consider how paltry this is in comparison to the thorny crown and the nails of Christ.

If you are obliged to do or to refrain from doing things against your will, ponder how Christ was captured and bound and led here and there.

If you are assailed by pride, see how your Lord was mocked and ridiculed along with criminals.

If unchastity and lust assail you, remember how bitterly Christ's tender flesh was scourged, pierced, and beaten.

If hatred, envy, and vindictiveness trouble you, recall how Christ, who indeed had more reason to avenge himself, interceded with tears and cries for you and for all his enemies.

If sadness or any adversity, physical or spiritual, distresses you, strengthen your heart and say, "Well, why should I not be willing to bear a little distress, when agonies and fears caused my Lord to sweat blood in the Garden of Gethsemane? Those who lay in bed while their Lord struggles in the throes of death are indeed lazy and disgraceful servants."

So then, this is how we find strength and encouragement from Christ against every vice and failing. This is the proper contemplation of Christ's passion, and such are its fruits. And those who exercise themselves in this way do better than listening to all the stories of Christ's passion or reading all the masses. This is not to say that masses are of no value, but they do not help us in this meditation and exercise.

Those who thus make Christ's life and name a part of their own lives are true Christians as St. Paul says [Gal 5:24], "Those who belong to Christ Jesus have crucified the flesh with its passions and desires." Christ's passion must be handled not with words or appearance but with life and truth. Thus St. Paul exhorts us [Heb 12:3], "Consider him who endured such hostility against himself from sinners, so that you may not grow weary or lose heart." And St. Peter writes [1 Pet 4:1], "Since therefore Christ suffered in the flesh, strengthen and arm yourselves by meditating on this." However, such meditation has gone out of fashion and become rare, even though the letters of St. Paul and St. Peter abound with it. We have transformed the essence into an appearance and have only painted our meditations on Christ's passion on walls and in pamphlets.

SERMONS ON THE SEVEN LAST WORDS

Mark 15:29–38 (Good Friday 2009)

Background for the Sermon

Preaching the law is not simply an opportunity to make people feel guilty. Instead, it means telling the truth about the human condition. In this sermon, the law arises through the simple question, And haven't we . . . ? Were the sermon simply directed at others, in this case at those most like "the Jews" or "the soldiers," it would become rank moralizing: "Don't be like them!" But finally to get to the "end" or goal of the law, our own religious avoidance comes into view. Once that great denial ("We are not like them") is named, other ways to interpret Jesus's words melt away, and justified sinners are left with the saving paradox of the text's actual words: "God ripping God's very self apart."[3]

The Sermon

Those in Jerusalem wanted a hero, someone who would rescue them from the oppressor's rod and win salvation glorious over the hated Roman army of occupation. And there he was, hanging on a Roman gallows between two bandits. They wanted a hero, but have there not been times when we wanted the same?

They wanted a sure, powerful sign from God, someone who would tear down buildings with his bare hands one day and build them up the next. And there he was, unable to move his hands or his feet. They wanted a sign, but have there not been times when we wanted the same?

They longed for Messiah, the King of Israel, the one anointed to bring in God's kingdom and power and glory and reestablish the throne of David. And there he was surrounded by taunts and mockery and derision, with the contemptuous charges scrawled above his head, "The King of the Jews." They wanted the chosen king, but have there not been times when we have longed for the same thing?

Worse yet, having heard this story of the crucified Messiah so many times, we face a far more troubling situation than those who first gathered around Christ's cross. We not only want a hero, a sign, and a ruler; we also want to avoid the scandal, the sheer scandal of the cross. While the other words from the cross may permit us to romanticize what happened that first Good Friday—allowing us to admire his heroic words to his mother; his forgiving words to his persecutors or the thief; his regal words of thirsting, finishing his atoning sacrifice, and commending his life to God. While the other words we hear and meditate on may allow us to duck the true awfulness of the crucifixion, these words of Jesus, the only ones recorded in the Gospel of Mark, will not.

"Eloi, Eloi, lema sabachthani?" The bystanders, of course, have

3. A line from Johannes Klaj cited in Udo Sträter, *Orthodoxie und Poesie* (Leipzig: Evangelische Verlagsanstalt, 2004).

their own brutal understanding of these words. They know the supposed sequence of events, rehearsed at the Passover meal the night before: first comes Elijah and then the Messiah. So they claim this faux-Messiah, this Jesus, calls out for Elijah to bring in the true Messiah. But they did not mishear what Jesus said; they only wanted to add to the derision. "Eloi" and "Eliya" are not the same words. And every good Hebrew- or Aramaic-speaking person knew what Jesus was quoting: Psalm 22, often the last words on a dying person's lips: "My God, my God, why have you forsaken me?" Calling for Elijah? Just more derision!

But we believers, like Mark's first readers, cannot make fun of these words—neither can we fathom the depth of the scandal occurring here. "My God, my God, why have you forsaken me?" This makes no sense! Mark tells us in no uncertain terms, in the very first verse of his Gospel, that this is "the good news [gospel] of Messiah Jesus, the Son of God" (Mark 1:1). And smack dab in the middle of the gospel, Peter names Jesus for who he is: "You *are* the Messiah!" (Mark 8:29). And at his trial, in the only words of Jesus recorded by Mark, Jesus answers the question whether he is Messiah, the Son of the Blessed One, with these words: "I am; and 'you will see the Son of Man seated at the right hand of the Power,' and 'coming with the clouds of heaven'" (Mark 14:62). It makes no sense. How can God's Son be abandoned by God?

Of course, Christian thinkers over the ages have tried to tone down these words of Jesus, domesticate them so that they fit our expectations. Accommodating teachers explain that Jesus's plea was simply the first words of a longer psalm that ends with hints of resurrection and would have been on the lips of every pious first-century Palestinian Jew at death. Or: He was saying it for our benefit and not speaking of himself at all. Or even: it proves Jesus was human.

All godly solutions to an ungodly scene! Pious platitudes designed to help us avoid the stark reality of the words or that imply at some level that all of that mockery was right: "My God, my God, why have you forsaken me?" Mark means for his readers to be confronted by the scandal of the cross and its foolishness. Here the only Son of God, the Messiah, actually cries out to God in complete dereliction! And, in case you miss the point, Mark records only a few verses later that one person—and the very last person we would suspect—gets the message, the point of the cross. For at the foot of the cross, the centurion, the Roman executioner, gasps, "Truly this man was God's Son" (Mark 15:39).

So, today, with all of our religious explanations swept away, we are left with the impossible: no sign, no wisdom, no power; only foolishness and weakness. What shall we say to this? As you know, I no longer preach for a living but instead teach at one of my church's seminaries. Since my specialty is the German Reformation of the sixteenth century, I am fluent in German. As a result, I often get the opportunity to review obscure books related to church history, including last year a book on seventeenth-century German religious poetry, some of whose work would later be immortalized by Johann Sebastian Bach in his famous chorales—one thinks of "O Sacred Head Now Wounded" or "Ah, Dearest Jesus," among others. Now, to be honest, I did not expect much from that little book and, as is often the case, I fussed and fumed over having agreed to review it in the first place. But then, about three-quarters of the way through that slim volume, I came across references to a German-speaking, Lutheran author who penned a series of poetic meditations on the last words of Jesus. One line of one of the poems on these words of Jesus jumped off the page and in an instant clarified exactly what Jesus was saying in our text.

"Es riß sich Gott von Gott." God is ripping God apart. That's the point. Here is not only a hero who dies a criminal's death, a sign of the prophet Jonah, or a crucified Messiah. Here is God ripped apart for our sake, for our sin, for our death, for our evil, for the cross we deserve. When Jesus spoke these words, he put an end to all of our most religious excuses and explanations of the cross and presented us with the scandal in which St. Paul gloried and in which we, too, may glory. God ripping God apart! It is not merely the temple curtain that is torn in two, but God. Indeed, the rending of the temple curtain is merely a visible sign of this divine action: God's heart pierced by the sword! Here is our God, in the very last place we would reasonably look, on the cross, dying for the sins of the world, our

sins—we who mock him and demand heroes, signs, and powerful rulers. "Behold, your king!" "Behold, your God, ripping his
heart in two for you, for me, for the whole world."

"Es riß sich Gott von Gott." God is ripping God apart. Here
might we stay and sing! God's life is ripped in twain! "In the
Cross of Christ I glory!" Here God's heart is truly broken!

> O sacred head, now wounded, with grief and shame weighed
>   down . . .
> be, Thou, my consolation, shield me when I must die.
> Remind me of your passion when my last hour draws nigh.
> Mine eyes shall then behold thee, upon Thy cross to dwell,
> my heart by faith enfold thee; who dieth thus dies well.

Luke 23:32–43 (Christ the King Sunday 2010)

Background for the Sermon

Nothing dulls preaching on the crucifixion more than when the
preacher downplays or neglects the scandal. In Luke, Christ rules
from the cross, truly the last place we would reasonably expect
to find God's Son. This scandal reveals sin in an instant, since
human life is filled with power grabs, manipulation, and claims
to righteousness and prosperity. But this very scandal of weakness *is* the gospel; the cross *is* Christ's throne, from which he
decrees forgiveness and eternal life.

Sermon

Whatever the condition of your heart or life today, whether you
came merely to celebrate the anniversary of this congregation
[Christ the King Lutheran Church, Houston, Texas] or out of
curiosity to see what a seminary professor looks like, whether
you are burdened with cares and sorrows, broken by economic
uncertainty or weighed down by concerns for your health, your
family, your job, or your country, I want you to know that you
could not have chosen a better day to come to worship than this
one, as we hear this gospel reading and discover its meaning for

our lives. Martin Luther, when preaching on part of this text in 1529, told his congregation, "Write this on your hearts with golden letters." Not bad advice at all.

Today is Christ the King Sunday. It was initiated among Roman Catholic Christians in 1925 as a way of trying to instruct governmental rulers how to act. But over the years, and especially as the feast was moved in the 1960s to the last Sunday of the church year and, in the 1970s, this gospel lesson was chosen to be read for this day in the year of Luke, it suddenly took on a wholly different meaning, even for Roman Catholics. This change was brought home to me last Friday evening. I teach a course at the seminary called the Inter-Seminary Seminar. It is held jointly with teachers and students from a Lutheran seminary, a Roman Catholic seminary, and a Baptist seminary. Students present papers on a single topic and discuss differences and similarities among their denominations. It has been in existence since 1959, the oldest continuously running, cooperative course in the United States. So on Friday, the conversation turned to how our various traditions understand Christ's mission on earth. And one particularly bright, jovial Roman Catholic seminarian said, "Well, it's like Luke 23 says, 'Christ the King rules from the cross.'" I thanked him afterward for giving me the theme for my sermon today. That's it. That's why we Lutherans have borrowed and helped transform this festival—so that no one ever forgets that the God we worship, Christ the King, rules not from a throne but from the cross.

One of Martin Luther's most important insights into Christian theology, one that has been used not only by Lutherans but also by many other Christian thinkers, is this: "God reveals himself in the last place we would reasonably look." And there is no place less reasonable to find God than on the cross, the Roman government's equivalent of the electric chair. Christ the King rules from the cross.

What a contrast to our own experience! We are surrounded by power grabs at every turn. Think about it. There are power struggles in our homes—whether it is a two-year-old's tantrum, a parent's explosive temper, the wheedling of a teenager, battles between spouses over who's in charge. There are struggles in the workplace: unfair bosses making outrageous demands; workers who react by doing less than they're required; companies that care only about the profit margin. There are struggles on the political front. We all hate attack ads, and yet they are the most effective way for politicians to get a leg up on their opponents. Everywhere we look, people demand control, power—even in our lives with God, we try to find ways to be in control. And look at Jesus's crucifixion. It is all about power: the power of Pilate and Jerusalem's religious leaders. The soldiers. Even the one thief wants a powerful God, saying in effect (cf. Luke 23:39): "If you are the chosen Messiah, the King, save yourself and us!" We are power addicts—whether we are passive, or passive-aggressive, or just downright aggressive. We all want control.

But I'm here to tell you the good news. Christ the King rules from the cross, the very last place anyone would expect to find the King of the universe. This King rules not with power but with weakness, not with wisdom but with foolishness, not with riches but in poverty, not by fighting to preserve his life but by giving his life up, by dying for us.

Think of what this means for your life and the life of your congregation! Think of it! Of all the consequences for this amazing good news, our story in Luke focuses especially on two things that this King-on-a-cross decrees, things that no one can ever take from you, no matter what happens. The first is simply this: "Father, forgive them; for they do not know what they are doing" (Luke 23:34). These are the words Martin Luther wanted his hearers to embroider on their hearts—and so do I! Why? Luther went on to say, "Include yourselves in the word 'them'!" When you look at the cross, where your sins drove Jesus, do not consider your sins so much as his forgiveness for you. On the cross that Good Friday, Jesus had you in mind, your sins, your carelessness, your lack of love for God or neighbor, your addiction to power and control. As king, he made an everlasting decree to his heavenly Father: "Father, forgive them!" He was thinking of you and you and you in that very moment, forgiving your sins, bearing them and taking them away. And, to this day, he continues to plead before the Father's throne: "Father, forgive her, forgive him; forgive them!"

Each time you witness a baptism and hear the child or adult's name joined to God's Triune name, then through the Holy Spirit you once again hear the Son's plea to the Father: "Father, forgive this child." And we return to that baptismal promise precisely when we confess our sins on Sunday morning and hear the pastor say that our sins are forgiven, not of his authority but by the authority of our crucified King. In fact, every time you ask God for forgiveness—as in the Lord's Prayer—then, too, our crucified King is praying, "Father forgive them!" We return to the same promises at the Lord's Table.

But, as if that weren't enough, our king gives a second decree from the throne of the cross, one that is even more powerful in its weakness. There they are, the three of them, hanging from crosses, dying. The one wants the kingdom, power, and glory. "If you're the king, start ruling the way a king should rule—get down from the cross for crying out loud and save us!" But then there is the other thief, who tells it like it is. "Do you not fear God, since you are under the same sentence of condemnation? And we indeed have been condemned justly, for we are getting what we deserve for our deeds, but this man has done nothing wrong" (Luke 23:40–41).

Sometimes, when I hear how some Christians think that religion is all about their getting and keeping power and, as they call it, "the abundant life" of riches, fame, health, and glory, then I think of this first thief and his addiction to power, his and our refusal to own up to the blatant truth: we are sinners who are getting what we deserve. But this crucified King has done nothing wrong. When we confess our sins each week, we are taking our place alongside the second thief, confessing the truth of our situation: "We are captive to sin and cannot free ourselves." When we face our own mortality or that of a loved one—when we realize that we cannot escape the sentence of death that is hanging over each one of us—then, too, we are hanging with that second thief, telling the truth about the mess we are in. We are justly condemned, justly dying, justly declared sinners. But this crucified King has done nothing wrong. "Jesus, remember me when you come into your kingdom" (Luke 23:42).

My dear friends, this is our only plea in the face of all the evil in this world, along with our sorrow, our anger, our sins, our dying. We have no claims to make; we are not in control; we have no power, and all of those things we invest with power and authority will finally not last. There is only one king, hanging in the last place we would reasonably look: on a cross—only one crucified King of the entire universe! To him we pray with that second thief, "Jesus, remember me when you come into your kingdom"!

And this king, this crucified Messiah, decrees and declares the most remarkable words in the entire Bible: "Truly I tell you, today you will be with me in Paradise"! Today! Mark that decree well when you grieve at the graveside over a loved one or even when you face your own death. Today! God's love is not broken by sin, for the King pleads for our forgiveness, and it is not broken by death, for this king declares, "Today!" We worship a crucified and risen King, who in the midst of sin and death and evil prepares a place for us in paradise. There is no better king, no more trustworthy ruler for your life and for your congregation than Christ, the crucified.

Luke 23:39–43 (Good Friday 2018)

Background for the Sermon

All kinds of characters in the biblical stories provide reflections of how the law condemns us. Here, where we would perhaps want to identify with the second, "good" thief, the story catches us doing or thinking, in one way or another, the very things the first thief says. Our self-centeredness knows no bounds. Only when the second thief proclaims the law ("Do you not fear God?") are we unmasked and forced to beg for mercy. Read the story any other way, and the sermon becomes another search for some moral agenda or another, and the preacher is forced to beg the hearers to be better. But the gospel, too, is not a way of escaping this life's crosses but a promise delivered to us while we are hanging on them. Again, the before-and-after understanding of sin disappears for the believing sinner.

Sermon

"One of the criminals . . . kept deriding him." And we, sanctimonious and self-assured Christians that we are, whisper, "Oh, that would never be me." Really? You see, the problem with hearing these seven last words is how quickly we, who know the end of the story and its empty tomb, want to be on the winning side. In the not-so-distant past, our churches may even have used the passion story to justify attacks on the Jewish people, quoting texts from this very story to justify such outrages. And yet, even though we may have stopped committing that sin against the cross, we still cook up others—especially when it comes to this second word of Jesus in Luke's passion narrative.

"One of the criminals . . . kept . . . saying, 'Are you not the Messiah? Save yourself and us!'" (Luke 23:39). Oh, no one who comes to church on a Friday afternoon would say such things, would they? And yet, and yet, when things go badly or even horrendously wrong on earth, do we not ask, "God, where are you?" or "If you are listening, God, why aren't you answering?" or "Save your reputation, and save us!" How many times aren't we the first thief on the cross—blaming God and putting God to the test, challenging God to get us out of the messes we find ourselves in?

Now do you smell the roast? In such circumstances, when this story turns sour and we are caught saying and thinking the words of the first thief on the cross, then the words of the second man catch us up short and knock us off our high horses. "Do you not fear God?" Then, and only then, when his words penetrate our hearts, do we find ourselves in the back of the temple—or the church—unable to look up to heaven and, like the tax collector in Luke 18, unable to say anything to God except, "God, be merciful to me, a sinner" (v. 13). Then, precisely when the rebuke of the second thief has its way with us, do we end up joining with him and saying, "For we are getting what we deserve for our deeds" (Luke 23:41). Enough of all this pious-sounding talk that Christians can earn favor, and long life, and earthly blessings. Enough of all of our complaining and whining! "We are getting what we deserve"—pain in childbirth, brokenness in families, thorns and thistles in the field, and sweat on your brow until we return to dust. Or, as Jesus says in Luke 13 in even stronger language than Genesis 3, towers falling on your head and your blood mixed with your sacrifices by a tyrant. Faced with such words of judgment from the mouth of that second thief, we can only dissolve in sorrow and sing, from "Rock of Ages," "Nothing in my hands I bring" and "Foul, I to thy fountain fly."

But there is another one who is with us as we sag under our weight on our crosses. And this other one, truly, has done nothing wrong. If there is anyone who should be complaining, it is him. Instead, as we heard in the first word from the cross in Luke, this one does not rail against his enemies, his crucifiers. Instead he prays forgiveness on them. Just forgives them! And then, once our empty railing against God has been revealed for what it truly is—lies and fakery—and we are confronted with our own complicity in our fate, what else can we do but cry out to this innocent one, "Jesus, remember me when you come into your kingdom"? For if you don't, who will?

We who lust after forcing God to justify our lot in life and what happens to us, are finally forced to our knees before this one whom the centurion, praising God, declares innocent. Then our prayer expands: "Nothing in my hands I bring; simply to thy cross I cling . . . Foul, I to thy fountain fly; wash me, Savior, or I die." You see, Augustus Toplady, that Anglican divine of eighteenth-century England, knew our situation too. And so in writing "Rock of Ages," he penned the perfect commentary on our situation, our place at the right and left hand of the crucified Messiah. "Lord, remember me when you come into your kingdom." Such a prayer of faith, you see, comes not out of the thief's strength but out of his weakness, his brokenness, and his desperation.

Remembrance appears twice in Luke's Gospel. The one comes from Jesus's command when, taking the bread and proclaiming it to be his body, he says, "Do this in remembrance of me" (Luke 22:19). Thus Christians the world over gathered yesterday to remember not ourselves but the one who makes us all new. And then here, in this text, we encounter not Jesus's command for us to remember but the thief's prayer to be remembered. And is that not a summary of all of our anguished prayers in this world? Your name be hallowed; your kingdom come; save us from trial; deliver us from evil (see Luke 11:2–4)? Father, keep me in mind! Jesus, remember me! Holy Spirit, do not forget me!

And then, in precisely that situation, in the midst of all of our pain and hopelessness and despair, we hear from the cross the one word we most desperately need to hear. "Truly I tell you, today you will be with me in Paradise" (Luke 23:43). Of course, as you may know, the word we translate as "truly" is the Hebrew word 'āmēn, as if Jesus were adding the amen to the thief's prayer—to our prayers. As one theologian put it, amen means nothing less than, "Yes, yes, it is going to happen just like that." "I will remember you!" But, as if that were not enough, Jesus said, "Today!" What a word in Luke! "For to you is born this day [today!], in the city of David, a savior, who is the Messiah, the Lord" (Luke 2:11). And in Jesus's first sermon, "Today this scripture has been fulfilled" (Luke 4:21). Or to Zacchaeus, "Today salvation has come to this house" (Luke 19:9).

Despite the way some religious demagogues talk about the end of the world and life after death, the Bible tells us surprisingly little about them. Paul says, "My desire is to depart and be with Christ, for that is far better" (Phil 1:23). And here, Jesus says, "Today you will be with me in Paradise." I stand before you as one widowed from his first wife, bereft of both parents. And I am here to tell you that these two verses contain enough comfort and tell us the one thing we most need to hear: in death those we love—better, those whom Jesus loves—will be with him "today." For this promise is for you and me and all with ears to hear, so that at our last hour we may hear these blessed words: "Today, today, you will be with me in Paradise." Having been expelled from Paradise by the first Adam, we will be welcomed by the second Adam to an even more blessed Paradise, "where," as John Doberstein prayed in *A Minister's Prayer Book*, "heart shall find heart, and those sundered on earth shall foregather in heaven" to be with Jesus, even today.

John 19:23–27 (Good Friday)

Background for the Sermon

The law shocks us out of our complacency and puts us in our place, but the more familiar we are with the passion story, the less it shocks us. By juxtaposing John's very different emphasis against the Synoptics, perhaps we can once again hear some of those very shocking things. But finally, to wring good news out of this strange encounter between Jesus and his mother, John's very language pushes the preacher toward what modern exegetes may dismiss as allegory but which is actually far closer to the Gospel writer's heart: From the cross, Jesus cares for his beloved disciple and his mother, that is, for the assembly of all believers we call the church.

Sermon

Aesop said it: "Familiarity breeds contempt." The fox is first afraid of the lion, then approaches him carefully, but by the third time is bold enough to chat him up. But such familiarity is much worse when it comes to the story of the passion. We have, over the centuries, managed to turn a Roman executioner's gallows into decoration to hang around our necks; we design Good Friday worship to play on our emotions; we skip Good Friday altogether in order to put on our Easter bonnets and sing our alleluias. We are so familiar with the story that its horror and scandal have escaped us completely.

It appears that John faced somewhat the same dilemma with his congregation, especially when we assume that he knew the standard stories, perhaps had even heard the other Gospels read aloud. So he must tell the story in such a way as to shock his listeners out of their complacency. For example, everyone knew that at the Last Supper Jesus took bread and wine and proclaimed them to be his body and blood. But John turns the story on its head, or rather on its feet, so that in the meal, at precisely the wrong time to wash feet, Jesus became the disciples' slave—pouring out his very self on their feet—the perfect icon of his Supper. No wonder early Christians called the Lord's Supper a *viaticum*, a picnic lunch—a washing of the feet for those weary on Christian life's journey toward Christ.

John faced the same problem in the passion story. He and his hearers know the basic story, so he concentrates on things we easily skip over. He hardly mentions Barabbas or the two thieves, but he takes the time to explain how offensive the sign over Jesus's head ("This is the King of the Jews") must have been to the temple leaders. "Write . . . 'This man said, I am the King of the Jews,'" they plead; to which Pilate replies, "What I have written I have written" (John 19:21–22).

By the time John writes his Gospel at the end of the first century, believers know to read the crucifixion in light of Psalm 22:

> They divide my clothes among themselves,
>   and for my clothing they cast lots. (v. 18)

But John has heard the complaints about enemies who had thrown his congregation out of their Greek-speaking synagogue: "If they divided the clothing, why would they cast lots? If they cast lots, why divide the clothing?" So he takes the time to explain how the four soldiers behaved: dividing up some but casting lots for something that couldn't be divided.

But then comes a story that no other Gospel mentions, a brief interaction between Jesus and his mother. Perhaps Psalm 22 was also in the back of John's mind:

> Yet it was you who took me from the womb;
>   you kept me safe on my mother's breast.
> On you I was cast from my birth,
>   and since my mother bore me you have been my God.

That very one who bore him and nursed him, standing by the cross with the beloved disciple—a silent testimony to the God who had taken Jesus from that womb, kept him safe, and was his God even on the cross. But what do we make of this scene? At first glance, we can praise Jesus for his filial piety, I suppose, especially when we realize that the word "woman" was scarcely an insult but rather a term of respect, so that we could almost translate it, "My Lady." We could thus praise Jesus for remembering his mother at the end of his life.

But even staying on this level, John invites us to delve deeper into the text, because this is only the second time that Jesus's mother appears in his Gospel. In John 2, when asking Jesus to help with the wine, he says to her, "What concern is that to you and me? My hour has not yet come" (v. 4). But now that hour has come, and the one from whose side will flow streams of living, life-giving water when the soldier pierces him with a spear is now ready to care for his mother by entrusting her to his beloved disciple.

But there is more. Outside of references in John to the woman at the well and Jesus's affectionate address to Mary Magdalene in the garden, there is one place where Jesus speaks of a woman, a woman in childbirth, and he uses her travail as a picture of his own death (John 16:21–22): "When a woman is in labor, she has pain, because her hour has come. But when her child is born, she no longer remembers the anguish because of the joy of having brought a human being into the world. So you have pain now; but I will see you again, and your hearts will rejoice, and no one will take your joy from you." Then we can see that the one who was in labor with Jesus is witness to his own moment of glory, his hour, and his birth to resurrection. "A sword will pierce your own soul too" (Luke 2:35).

But John is not done with us yet. He pushes us yet further into the mystery of the cross. His language throughout his Gospel will not allow us to sleep. Water into wine becomes a sign of his glory; the miracle of bread tells us Jesus is the bread of life; the raising of Lazarus reveals Jesus the resurrection and the life. And here? Is it just that Jesus is a good son? That he knows all of Psalm 22? That John would underscore the connection between labor pains and Jesus's death? Perhaps, but perhaps John forces us to admit something even more remarkable: that the mother of Jesus is also the mother of all the faithful, who live in hope of Jesus's glorious hour and in the travail of his cross. Then the beloved disciple is precisely all of those disciples who bring the faithful into their house.

Under everything, you see, this is a perfect picture of the church—of you and me, standing as we do right now under the cross as believers and being given into the care of the beloved disciple—who, like Andrew, says to Peter, "We have found the Messiah!" (John 1:41) or, like Philip, says to Nathanael, "We have found him about whom Moses and the prophets wrote!" (John 1:45) or, like the Samaritan woman, says to her village, "He told me everything I have ever done!" (John 4:29) or, like the blind man, says to the Pharisees, "Though I was blind, now I see!" (John 9:25) or, beautifully like Mary Magdalene, at the cross and the empty tomb, an apostle sent to tell the apostles, "I have seen the Lord!" (John 20:18).

Who could believe it? This passion story, so well known to every Christian community, is not simply a quaint story of past injustice at the hands of the powerful; not a story to evoke nostalgia; not designed to pay off God or move you to feel bad about your sins. In John's new perspective, this is a story about the immeasurable love of Jesus for his beloved mother and his beloved disciple—that is, it is all about Jesus's love for you in the family and house of God. As we stand in the midst of travail, in labor for an end to evil and sin, to injustice and death, Jesus speaks, here and now, to us, the weeping faithful waiting for the joy and elation of new birth. Here is your family, your son and daughter, who, like John the Baptist, will point to the Lamb of God who takes away the sin of the world. After all, there is for the evangelist a witness that Jesus's bones, like the Paschal Lamb, were not broken and that blood and water—Supper and baptism—flow from his wounded side. That is the witness of every beloved disciple of every age. "Woman, behold your son, your daughter." "Children, behold your mother." Ah, dear Christians, this is our house, our home, our mother, and our beloved disciple. But, for those in travail, yearning for the end, this is our beloved Savior of the world, Messiah, Son and Word of God. And, even and especially from the cross, in his glory, he gives us, who are homeless, a home. For John, familiarity breeds family, a home for us with God.

John 19:28–37 (Good Friday 2011)

Background for the Sermon

The tradition of dividing up each and every word of Jesus fails in John, where the two last words of Jesus form a matching set. John the master theologian accepts the challenge of our questions and our vulnerabilities. This kind of dialogical paraphrase ("I thirst . . . It is finished"), of which Luther was so fond, drives us deeper into the text and forces us (as the law is wont to do) to "streams of living water" flowing from his wounded side. Preaching the gospel is always turning the text toward the hearers, so that they hear, "Here is Christ for you," so that faith is born from above.

Sermon

If Mark invented the form of prose we call "Gospel"; if Matthew linked that form to the central truth that Jesus is Immanuel, God with us; and if Luke is the master storyteller among the Gospel writers; then John is the master theologian, taking the story and reminding us with every stroke of the pen what this story is all about—why Christians around the world gather on these three days to proclaim, "Christ has died; Christ is risen; Christ will come again."

"'It is finished,' hear him cry; learn of Jesus Christ to die." As profound as those words of James Montgomery, in "Go to Dark Gethsemane," are, still they only scratch the surface of John's story. But when we combine this sixth word of Jesus with the previous word, "I thirst," what would have jumped out at the original Greek readers was this: John repeats the same word three times in fewer than four lines. "After this, when Jesus knew that all was now *fulfilled*, he said (in order to *fulfill* the Scripture), 'I am thirsty.' . . . When Jesus had received the wine, he said, 'It is *fulfilled*'" (John 19:28–30). Fulfilled, finished, completed, ended!

But what is done, dear John? How do you understand the words that you have written, the story that you are telling? To help us with these curious, cryptic words, John then describes in great detail what happened next. Apparently, he knew that the way to hasten death in such gruesome situations was to break the victims' legs, thereby shocking them to death. But Jesus had already given up his spirit, John writes, and so they simply pierced his side, and out poured blood and water. This event is so important for John that he adds his own bona fide: "He who saw this has testified so that you also may believe. His testimony is true, and he knows that he tells the truth" (John 19:35). And then he tells us why, using that same Greek verb for a fourth time: "These things occurred so that the scripture might be *fulfilled*: 'None of his bones shall be broken.' And again another passage of scripture says, 'They will look on the one whom they have pierced'" (vv. 36–37).

It is finished. That is, it's all over but the shouting. If, somehow, you had missed the five words that preceded this one or needed to slip out the back before you hear the last word, you have, in John's view, heard it all. The whole point of Jesus's death, the whole point of Jesus's life and John's Gospel, the whole point of your life and mine comes to completion in these few words. As John tells us here, it truly is finished, completed, fulfilled in three remarkable ways.

Let's begin with the verse "None of his bones shall be broken." No, not one! The passage is from Exodus 12 and refers to the Passover lamb. For John this is so important that he changes slightly the date of the crucifixion so that Jesus dies exactly at the time when the priests were busy in the temple slaughtering lambs for Passover. And as soon as we realize these things, we also know why John quotes it here. The lamb has already been mentioned once in the Gospel, way back at the beginning, when John the Baptist points to Jesus and twice says to his disciples, "Behold the Lamb of God!" (John 1:29 KJV). No wonder that nearly from that day to this, Christians have sung, "Lamb of God, have mercy!" and "O Christ, you Lamb of God who takes away the sin of the world, have mercy," or now as a more recent song has it, "Now behold the Lamb, the precious lamb of God."

For Christians of the Middle Ages, this was so important that they often depicted the crucifixion with John the Baptist at the foot of the cross, holding a lamb and pointing to Christ. Thus, too, for us! If you come this afternoon burdened with sins, anxious with cares, here is the Lamb of God, who takes away the sin of the world. We need celebrate Passover no longer, for Christ our Passover Lamb has been sacrificed for us—once and for all. Sin is finished! Grace is fulfilled!

But there is still more. For from the side of this thirsty, dying one comes blood and water. Water! Remember the woman at the well and what Jesus said to her? "If you knew the gift of God, and who it is that is saying to you, 'Give me a drink,' you would have asked him, and he would have given you living water" (John 4:10). And then, in a still more shocking scene several chapters later, Jesus interrupts the procession at the Feast of Booths in Jerusalem, just when the high priest is carrying the golden pitcher of water from one of the springs to pour on the altar, this Lamb of God and Light of the World cries out, "Let anyone who is thirsty come to me, and let the one who believes in me drink. As the scripture has said, 'Out of his belly shall flow rivers of living water'" (John 7:37–38).[4] Out of the belly, the wounded side, of this thirsty one, flow rivers of living water! John is witness to this remarkable fact. Leave your biology at the door; do not waste time imagining the excruciating suffering of Christ. Rather, come to his cross and receive, thirsty one, living, flowing water and blood—water at the font of baptism and blood at his Table. All of it flowing for you for forgiveness, life, and salvation! It is finished; all is fulfilled; the floodgates of God's infinite, never-failing mercy have burst open from his belly, his side, and the Word made flesh now gives up his flesh for the life of the world—for your life, for mine. Thirst is finished! Life is fulfilled!

And yet there is one more surprising gift, one more amazing fulfillment in this text for us today: "Then he bowed his head and gave up his spirit" (John 19:30). His Spirit! Again, in that remarkable text from chapter 7, John explains that living water this way: "Now he said this about the Spirit, which believers

---

4. Translated from the original Greek and not using the somewhat garbled NRSV translation.

in him were to receive; for as yet the Spirit was not yet given, because Jesus was not yet glorified" (John 7:39, author's translation). But here, on the cross, he gives up his Spirit, and three days later, this one still with wounded hands and feet and side will breathe on his disciples and say, "Receive the Holy Spirit" (John 20:22). The gift of the Holy Spirit comes precisely in Jesus's glorification, that is, in his death and resurrection. Indeed, there is no Spirit, no church, no gospel, no hope, and—most importantly—no faith outside the death and resurrection of this one, who is Word, Lamb, and Water of Life. Indeed, this text and this gospel are all about the faith this Spirit-giving Savior provides. For to Nicodemus, who will bury him in the verses after our text, Jesus talked of a person being "born from above . . . by water and the Spirit" (cf. John 3:3, 5). That is to say, our birth from above, from God, is a matter of the water of Jesus's wounded side and the Spirit he gave up on the cross. Our faith is a matter of his death for us. There, on the cross, all is finished, all is completed, all is fulfilled—for you, for me, and for all. Unbelieving is finished! Faith is fulfilled!

"It is finished!" is a single, simple word in Greek. And yet this one word offers forgiveness of sin from the Lamb, an end to all thirst from the one who gives living water, and the beginning of faith, true faith from the one who bears us from above on the cross. *Tetelestai.* It is truly all over but the shouting, the praising, the thanksgiving, and the grateful songs. "Here might I stay and sing," the poet Samuel Crossman said in "My Song Is Love Unknown." And another, "Ah, Holy Jesus," "Ah, dearest Jesus, since I cannot pay thee, I will adore thee and forever pray thee, think on thy mercy and thy love unswerving, not my deserving." Now, on the cross, everything God wills for the human race, for you, is fulfilled, is completed. Your thirst is quenched! It is finished!

Luke 23:44–49 (Good Friday)

Background for the Sermon

The Renaissance interest in the *argumentum*, or central point, of a text or book of the Bible has allowed exegetes ever since to open up the meaning of the Gospels. But what Luther, Melanchthon, and their colleagues achieved was a unique look at the centrality of the relation between God's promise and faith. Luke's Gospel has a collection of Jesus's sayings where he calls on God as Father. This remarkable word is on Jesus's lips in his first words and in his last. For Luke, the word is neither ontologically conditioned nor socially restricted but, as Melanchthon realized with the word *justification*, relationally understood. And that relationship reveals the good news of Jesus, who is, as Luther said, "the mirror of the Father's heart."

Sermon

Famous last words! Wolfgang Goethe, the famous German writer, cried out, "More light!" John Adams, dying on the Fourth of July, whispered, "Jefferson still lives!" And, of course, there was Louis XV, whose successor would die at the guillotine, "After me, the deluge!" So it goes! Early Lutherans, too, strained to hear the last words of the Reformers. Luther confessed his faith and left, as his last written words, this remarkable confession mixing German and Latin: *Wir sind Bettler; hoc est verum* (We are beggars; this is true). And his companion Philip Melanchthon was said to have recited over and over, "If God is for us, who can be against us?"

Much earlier in the church's history, the author of the book of Acts in the New Testament records Stephen's last words as he is being stoned to death: "Lord Jesus, receive my spirit" and "Lord, do not hold this sin against them," painting the picture of a good Christian death, confessing one's faith (Acts 7:59–60). But, of course, Stephen was simply echoing Jesus's words in Luke. This leads us, finally, to Jesus's last words. Each Gospel writer has his favorites. Matthew and Mark content themselves with Psalm 22: "My God, my God, why have you forsaken me?" (Matt 27:46; Mark 15:34). John begins with remarkable words to Mary and the beloved disciple, before reflecting another verse in Psalm 22 ("I am thirsty," John 19:28) and "It is finished" (John 19:30). But Luke concentrates on other words: first a prayer of forgiveness for his executioners (like Stephen's); then a promise to the thief on the cross; but finally, quoting Psalm 31, Jesus's last words.

Doubtless Luke knew Mark's shocking last words of dereliction. Perhaps he realized that people in his congregation had misunderstood Mark's intent and wondered, as do we, how God could possibly abandon God's Son. So he searched for another Psalm that made the same point, but in a kinder, gentler form. The point of reciting Psalm 22 really was the same as the point behind Psalm 31:

> Into your hand I commit my spirit;
>> you have redeemed me, O Lord, faithful God. (v. 5; cf.
>> Luke 23:46)

Luke's point throughout the passion narrative is to show Jesus's innocence, which is the intent of both Psalm 22 and especially Psalm 31, underscored through the declaration of Jesus's innocence by the thief and the centurion.

This speculation could be true, but it may miss the point that, of all the words Jesus could have used, of all the psalms he could have cited, when he breathed his last Jesus had nothing more to say to us but instead breathed himself into his Father's hands. Perhaps James Montgomery was right in "Go to Dark Gethsemane": "Learn of Jesus Christ to die." Even more than the depictions of Christ's passion in the other three Gospels, Luke's is filled with other players: Pilate, Herod, and the religious leaders; Simon of Cyrene, wailing women from Jerusalem, soldiers, the centurion, crowds beating their breasts, and, at a distance, Jesus's acquaintances, including the women. But it is the last three—the rueful crowd, the confessing centurion, and Jesus's acquaintances and supportive Galilean women—who witness these last words.

What do we learn about dying from this last word? Everything hinges not so much on the psalm he recited as on the first word of his prayer not in the Psalm: "Father!" What a word for Jesus in Luke: "Did you not know," the twelve-year-old Jesus exclaimed in the temple, "that I must be in My Father's house?" (Luke 2:49). And so he encouraged his followers to be merciful, "as your Father is merciful" (6:36); and he insisted that the "Son of Man" will come in "the glory of the Father" (9:26). "Have no fear, little flock, it is the Father's good pleasure to give you the kingdom" (cf. 12:32; ELW 764). But more importantly, in Luke's Gospel Jesus prays to the Father, thanking him for having hidden these things from the wise and having revealed them to children, for "no one knows . . . who the Father is except the Son" (10:22). And, of course, he begins the most famous prayer of all with the word "Father," the parent who knows what we need and is more likely to give the Holy Spirit than earthly fathers give good things to their children. And in Gethsemane, "Father, if you are willing . . ." (22:42). And on the cross: "Father, forgive them . . ." (23:34).

And so, at the end, because there is no one else on whom to rely, no other God, this righteous, innocent one, this Son of the Most High, cries out, "Father, into your hands I commend my spirit." If the cross in Mark's Gospel rips God's heart in two, here the cross unites the Father and the Son in a death that leads to resurrection. But the heart of both Gospels lays bare the Father's heart, not just for Jesus's sake but also for ours. This Father will not give scorpions or stones for eggs and bread, but will give the very Holy Spirit coming forth from the one who committed his spirit to the Father. This one will not leave his foolish, weak children orphaned but will hear their every cry, our every cry, even in the face of death. This God will empower our dying so that, in the power of the Holy Spirit and by faith alone, our last words can only be: "Father, into your hands we commend our spirit. For there are no other hands than yours, and your Son's ever-wounded hands prove your mercy."

5.

Living with the Saints in the Psalms

In 1546, the Smalcald War broke out, and Wittenberg was besieged. Luther had already died, but many were afraid what would happen to his wife, Katharina von Bora, in the event of the city's capitulation (which occurred in 1547). So Philip Melanchthon set out with his family and hers, the group becoming refugees in the midst of the chaos of war. Melanchthon later reported that Katharina told him that she had never understood the psalms of lament until that time of distress. Hundreds of years later, Dietrich Bonhoeffer reported a similar experience. And in the 1990s, Prof. Michael Möller, my colleague at the Lutheran Theological Seminary at Philadelphia, reflected on his experience while a resistance pastor in the German Democratic Republic, where—forbidden to preach—congregants assembled on Sunday evenings to hear and recite the Psalter. A more powerful sermon could not have been given at the time!

The psalms constitute the most remarkable book of the Bible, because they reflect absolutely every emotion of the believer—from joy to sorrow, from trust to doubt, from lament to thanksgiving. Luther's interpretations of the psalms reflect this variety, as he recognized the "faithful synagogue" praying the psalms alongside him and Christ and as he continued to expand on a tradition begun by Augustine in his sermons on the psalms from a thousand years earlier. This chapter begins with Luther's famous preface to the Psalter from his German translation of the Bible. It includes for each psalm a translation of the appropriate comments from Luther's *Summaries of the Psalms* from 1531–1533, as well as (on occasion) other insights from Luther.

This chapter also includes recent reflections by the author of this book, echoing many of Luther's exegetical and hermeneutical insights (although at the time I wrote them, I was unfamiliar with Luther's *Summaries*). It intends to lead the reader into the psalms anew but from the very specific perspective of suffering and death, closely related to Luther's rejection of "before-and-after" exegesis (since "dying we live" is simply another aspect of the *simul iustus et peccator*). These meditations began their life as daily morning emails to the author's daughter Emily, written to her while she attended college and based on the particular psalm that the author and his wife, Barbara, who was then struggling with cancer, had read the evening before. Emily preserved them, edited them, and gave them back to me as a Christmas present that year (2000), only five months before her mother finally succumbed to the disease on May 18, 2001.[1]

MARTIN LUTHER'S PREFACE TO THE PSALTER
FROM 1528 (1545)

Many holy Fathers praised and loved the Psalter above all other books of Scripture.[2] To be sure, the work itself gives enough praise to its author [God]. We, however, must give evidence of our own praise and thanks.

In years past, so many legends of the saints, and passionals, books of examples, and histories have been circulated that the world has been so filled with them. Hence, the Psalter has lain under the bench and in such obscurity that no one has understood even one psalm correctly. Still the Psalter gave off such an exquisitely excellent scent that all pious hearts felt the devotion and power in the unknown words, and for this reason loved the book.

I hold, however, that no finer book of examples or of legends

1. The author's father, who was suffering from Alzheimer's and figures in one of the meditations, died the following July.
2. AL 6:206–12 (WA Bi 10/1:98–104).

of the saints has ever come—or can come—to earth than the Psalter. If one should wish that from all the examples, legends, and histories, the best should be selected and brought together and put in the best form, the result would have to be the present Psalter. For here we find not only what one or two saints have done, but what has been done by the one who is at the very head of all saints [Christ]. We also find what all the saints still do—such as the attitude they take toward God, toward friends and enemies, and the way they conduct themselves in all dangers and sufferings. Beyond that there are contained here all sorts of godly and healing teachings and commandments.

The Psalter ought to be a dear and beloved book, if only because it promises Christ's death and resurrection so clearly—and pictures Christ's kingdom and the condition and nature of all Christendom—that it might well be called a little Bible. The Psalter puts everything that is in the entire Bible most beautifully and briefly; it is truly a fine *enchiridion* or handbook. It seems to me that the Holy Spirit wanted to take the trouble to compile a short Bible and example book of all Christendom or of all saints, so that whoever could not read the whole Bible would have here almost an entire summary of it, comprised in one little booklet.

But above all this, the Psalter has this excellent virtue and manner: other books make much ado about the works of the saints, but say very little about their words. The Psalter is a gem in this respect: it gives forth so sweet a scent when one reads it because it related not only the works of the saints, but also their words—how they spoke with God and prayed, and still speak and pray. Compared to the Psalter, the other legends and examples present to us nothing but merely speechless saints; the Psalter, however, pictures for us real, thoroughly living saints.

Compared to a speaking person, a speechless one is to be regarded simply as a half-dead person: and there is no mightier or nobler work of humanity than speech. A human person is most differentiated from other animals by speech, much more than by a human person's shape or any other work. By the woodcarver's art even a block of wood can be given the shape of a human person; and an animal can see, hear, smell, sing, walk, stand, eat, drink, fast, thirst, hunger, and even suffer from frost and a hard bed—as much as a human person.

Moreover, the Psalter does still more than this. It presents to us not the simple, ordinary speech of the saints, but the best of their speech, that which they used when they spoke with God in great earnestness and on the most important matters. Thus, the Psalter lays before us not only their words instead of their works, but their very hearts and the inmost treasure of their souls, so we can look down to the foundation and source of their words and works. We can look into their hearts and see what kind of thoughts they had, how their hearts were disposed, and how they acted in all kinds of situations, in danger and in need. The legends and examples, which boast only of the works and miracles of the saints, do not and cannot do this, for I cannot know how a person's heart is, even though I see or hear of many important works this person does. And just as I would rather hear what a saint says than see the works the saint does, so I would much rather see the saint's heart and the treasure in the saint's soul than hear the saint's words. And this the Psalter gives us most abundantly concerning the saints, so that we can be certain of how their hearts were towards God and of the words they expressed to God and to everyone.

A human heart is like a ship on a wild sea, driven by storm winds from the four corners of the world. Here it is struck with fear and worry about coming disaster; there comes grief and sorrow because of present evil. Here it floats on hope and anticipated good fortune; there blows confidence and joy in present blessings. These storm winds teach us to speak earnestly, to open the heart and pour out what lies at the bottom of it. The person who is stuck in fear and need speaks of misfortune very differently than the one who floats on joy; and the one who floats on joy speaks and sings of joy quite differently from the one who is stuck in fear. It is not from the heart, they say, when a sad person laughs or a glad person weeps. That is, the bottom of the heart is not open, and what is in it does not come out.

What is the greatest thing in the Psalter but this earnest speaking amid such storm winds of every kind? Where does one find finer words of joy than in the praise psalms and thanksgiving psalms? There you look into the hearts of all the saints, as into beautiful and pleasant gardens—yes, as into heaven itself. There you see what fine and pleasant flowers of the heart spring up from all sorts of beautiful and happy thoughts toward God, because of God's blessings.

On the other hand, where do you find deeper, more sorrowful, more pitiful words of sorrow than in the lamentation psalms? There you look into the hearts of all the saints, as into death—yes, as into hell. How gloomy and dark it is there, with all kinds of distressed forebodings about the wrath of God! So, too, when they speak of fear and hope, they use such words that no painter could so depict for you fear or hope, and no Cicero or other orator so portray them.

And that they speak these words to God and with God, this, I repeat, is the best thing of all. This gives the words double earnestness and life. For when one speaks with human persons about these matters, what he or she says does not come so powerfully from the heart; it does not burn and live, is not so urgent. Hence, it is that the Psalter is the book of all saints; and everyone, in whatever situation that person may be, finds in the psalms words that fit his or her case or situation—that suit him or her as if they were put there just for his or her sake, so that they could not put it better themselves, or find better words or wish for better.

And this, too, is good that when these words please a person and suit her or his case, this person becomes sure that they are in the communion of saints, and that it has gone with all the saints as it goes with him or her self, since they all sing with this person one little song. It is especially so if this person can speak these words to God as they [the saints] have done. This must happen in faith since these words have no flavor to a godless human being.

Finally, there is in the Psalter security and a well-tried guide, so that one can follow in it all the saints without peril. The other examples and legends of the speechless saints present works that one cannot imitate; they present even more works that are dangerous to imitate—works that usually start sects and fierce divisions, and lead away from the communion of saints and rip it apart. But the Psalter holds you away from the divisions and to the communion of saints. For it teaches you—in joy, fear, hope, and sorrow—to contemplate and speak as all the saints have contemplated and spoken.

In summary, if you would see the holy Christian church painted with living color and shape and put into one little picture, then take up the Psalter. There you have a fine, bright, pure mirror that will show you what Christendom is. Indeed you also will find yourself in it and the true *gnothiseauton* [know yourself], as well as find God in God's very self and all creatures.

Let us see to it then also that we thank God for all these unspeakable blessings. Let us receive them and use them diligently and earnestly, exercising ourselves in them to God's praise and honor, lest we earn something worse with our ingratitude. Heretofore, in the time of darkness, what a treasure it would have been thought if one were able to understand a psalm correctly and to read or hear it in understandable German, but we did not have that treasure. Yet now, blessed are the eyes that see what we see and the ears that hear what we hear [Luke 10:23]. And yet I fear—no, sad to say, we see—that things happen with us as with the Jews in the wilderness, when they spoke about the bread from heaven [Num 21:5]: "We detest this miserable food." We should remember, however, that alongside this story there also stands the story of how they were plagued and died, lest the same thing happen to us.

To this may the Father of all grace and mercy help us, through Jesus Christ our Lord, to whom be praise and thanks, honor and glory, for this German Psalter and for all God's innumerable and unspeakable blessings into eternity. Amen, amen.

PSALMS FOR THE SORROWFUL

Psalm 1

From Martin Luther's *Summaries of the Psalms*

The First Psalm is a psalm of comfort. It admonishes us that we should eagerly hear and learn God's Word, and it comforts us that we have great and many blessings from this, namely, that all of our words and works shall be divinely supported in the face of all possible enemies, just as a palm tree on the water's edge stays green and bears fruit in the face of all kinds of heat and frost and the like. The teaching of human beings does not do this. Instead, just as the wind blows the chaff away, they pass away too. For God is pleased with these students of his word (he says), but he lets the others pass away. And this psalm flows out of the third commandment and belongs to it, because that commandment to celebrate the Sabbath means eagerly to hear and learn God's Word. And this psalm is comprehended in the Lord's Prayer, in the second and third petitions, where we pray about God's kingdom and will, both of which are furthered through his Word.[3]

Meditation: "Walking by Faith Alone"

This psalm forms a preface or introduction to the entire Psalter. It presents the grand contours of the lives of faith and unbelief. For the first verse, the New International Version (1984) is more faithful to the Hebrew imagery.

> Blessed is the man
> who does not walk in the counsel of the wicked
> or stand in the way of sinners
> or sit in the seat of mockers. (v. 1)

It is about "the man" (as in male), since at this time it was the men who read the Torah and the Psalms. Today we can say (as in the NRSV) "those who" and include all of us. But notice the interesting development from "walk" to "stand" to "sit" and also from "the counsel of the wicked," "the way of sinners," and to "the seat of mockers." The first is a matter of following bad advice, the second of frequenting bad places, and the third as being completely at one with those who want nothing to do with God. See? It is faith (or unbelief) alone that makes a god. Whom do you trust? Whose advice do you follow? Where do you walk? With whom do you sit?

---

3. WA 38:18, 15–27. His comments about the third commandment and the second and third petitions of the Lord's Prayer reflect his exposition of them in the 1529 catechisms. This and the following translations by the author.

> But his delight is in the law of the Lord,
>   and on his law he meditates day and night. (v. 2)

It is the *Torah*, the first five books of the Bible, that is translated "law." By the time this psalm was written (relatively late, say, around 400 BC or so), the Torah was the center of Jewish life, as it still is today. Luther notes in his earliest lectures on the Psalms that it says here his delight is in the law of the Lord and *not* the law of the Lord is in his delight. That is, this reader shapes what he delights by the law and not the other way around, where we try to make God and God's Word match our expectations. So often that selfish mentality is all you hear about in the church.

But also notice that the word *Torah* here does not simply mean "rules and regulations" but really is a synonym for God's Word and will.

> He is like a tree
>   planted by streams of water,
> which yields its fruit in season
>   and whose leaf does not wither.
> Whatever he does prospers. (v. 3)

And so it is that you and I read psalms and sing hymns and gain strength from the tree of life.

> Not so the wicked!
>   They are like chaff that the wind blows away.
> Therefore, the wicked will not stand in the judgment,
>   nor sinners in the assembly of the righteous. (vv. 4–5)

Maybe this is the origin of the "Three Little Pigs." What happens when you build your house of straw? Or, more likely, it is the origin of Paul's line about how some teachers build on Christ's foundation with gold but others with wood and straw. And, if the latter, when a fire comes, the straw and wood will be consumed. Luther, reading the Letter of James, called it *ein recht strohende Epistel* (a real strawy epistle). The closer to the streams of water, that is, God's Word of grace, the more we prosper. That is for sure. The farther away and the more we have to rely

on ourselves, the more it is certain we will dry up and blow
away.

> For the Lord watches over the way of the righteous,
>   but the way of the wicked will perish. (v. 6)

The Jewish scholars call instruction *halakah*, which is the same
word as "road" or "way." Notice how often that metaphor comes
up in this psalm. Walking in something is *not* the same as doing
something; it has much more to do with trust. The notion of
the Lord watching over a way is so beautiful. There is One who
knows, whose "eye is on the sparrow, and I know he watches
me," as the spiritual goes. Thanks be to God!

Prayer: Dear God, keep us in your way so that our lives may
bear good fruit, through Christ our Lord. Amen.

Psalm 6

From Martin Luther's *Summaries of the Psalms*

The Sixth Psalm is a prayer psalm and laments over the high
and truly secret suffering of the conscience, which, because of its
sins, is martyred by the law and wrath of God and driven into
doubt or false belief. Otherwise the Psalter calls this in various
places "the bands of death" and "the cords of hell" or "the threat
of death" or the "fear of hell." But in the end the psalmist shows
that such a prayer is heard as a comforting example to all who
are under similar attack [*Anfechtung*]: that they shall not remain
therein. And the psalm reprimands evildoers, that is, false saints,
who generally hate such downcast people and persecute them.
For their comfort consists in their own holiness, and they know
nothing of such attacks. For this reason they are the worst enemies of pure faith. This psalm belongs to the first and second
commandment, because it praises the struggle of believing in
God and prays against sin and death. And, like all other psalms,

it is in the first petition of the Lord's Prayer, because to pray is to call on and honor God's name.[4]

Meditation: "Deliver Us from Evil"

This psalm is short, sweet, and to the point. In *Today's English Version* we read: "Lord, don't be angry and rebuke me! Don't punish me in your anger! Have pity on me, because I am worn out; restore me, because I am completely exhausted." The request is simple: "Deliver us from evil." We want rescue, and we want it quickly.

Seen from this life (which is the gift of God we have now), corpses offer no praise. The Hebrews had little concept of life after death. But then, neither do we. In Christ, all we have is a promise that where he is we will be also. In any case, it is not wrong to concentrate on this life and ask for mercy and healing here. It is, after all, a good life.

> I am worn out with grief;
>> every night my bed is damp from my weeping,
>> my pillow is soaked with tears. (v. 6)

Now, thank God, we do not carry on quite like the psalmist. But there are times. A youngster at Cross Lutheran Church[5] sent Mom a blanket signed by many of its members, and she burst into tears at the sentiment.

> Keep away from me, you evil people!
> The Lord hears . . .
>> he listens . . .
>> and will answer my prayer. (vv. 8–9)

That's all we have in the end, Emily: faith alone. Trust that God will in the end act—either in this life or at the resurrection—it doesn't matter. But in the end, the enemies, even death, will be defeated. That is what Easter and the hope it brings are all about.

---

4. WA 38:20, 3–17.

5. The congregation in Roberts, Wisconsin, where the author served as pastor from 1983 to 1989.

Even weeping—which has no words—is a poignant prayer to God.

Prayer: Dear God, you know our hearts; you hear our cries. Answer them for the sake of our risen Savior, Jesus Christ our Lord. Amen.

Psalm 13

From Martin Luther's *Summaries of the Psalms*

The Thirteenth Psalm is a prayer psalm against the sadness or heavy burdens of the spirit. Sometimes it comes from the devil himself; sometimes also from other people, who take action against us with evil malice and schemes, so that we end up becoming saddened when we see such great evil arrayed against us. But prayer is stronger than all misfortune, as this psalm gives an example of, so that we should certainly be comforted and learn in all kinds of tragedies not to be troubled, saddened, or bite and devour ourselves in our hearts. Instead, we should stick to praying and complain to God about all such matters, certain that we will be heard and, in the end, redeemed, as Saint James also says [Jas 5:13]: "If someone is downcast, let him pray." This psalm belongs to the second commandment and in the first and last petitions, where we pray to be delivered from evil.[6]

Meditation: "Faith's Lament"

Psalm 13 is a song of lament. It is even written in a different meter from the praise songs. The latter go 3 3 (emphasized syllables per phrase), whereas the laments are most often a more "limping" 3 2. And Psalm 13 is among the most pointed—I was going to say saddest, but that honor goes to Psalm 88. So I asked Mom how she felt, and she said frustrated. This psalm fits the bill. Actually, in his preface to the book of Psalms in the German translation, Luther talks about how the heart is like a ship on the ocean. Sometimes it is riding the crest of the waves, and some-

6. WA 38:22, 8–19.

times it is deep in a trough. The psalms reflect every emotion of the human heart: from praise and jubilation to quiet trust; from questioning to lament and sorrow and even despair.

Here you look into the heart of the saints, Luther continues. When they are praising, it is a beautiful garden like paradise itself. When they are sad, it is like gazing into hell. Yet all of these emotions and feelings are sanctified by the Holy Spirit, who inspired these prayers. Sometimes people think they have to pretend to be strong in order to pray. The psalms give us permission to be honest with God. He can take our anger, doubts, and disappointments better than anyone else. So here the psalmist asks, "How long?" For us it is almost two months since we heard the diagnosis [January 15, 2000] and at least four months since we started the tests. But it is not just "How long the chemotherapy?" (although that's part of it), but "How long will you forget me?" No matter how strong your faith, sometimes we feel as though God has forgotten us (or, as in Psalm 22, prayed by Jesus on the cross, forsaken us). It is as though God has hidden himself—nowhere more than on the cross itself—but also in such a horrible illness.

Doesn't God care? The fact is that such an event brings searing pain and sorrow in one's heart all day long (v. 2). I know you know, Emily, what this feels like—imagine for me or much more for Mom herself. There are always enemies in these psalms. These are self-righteous people who (whether they mean to or not) look down their noses at those who suffer. I had one such student, who volunteered to lay his hands on Mother because he had the gift of healing. What arrogance! And after I had just begged students just to be students. God knows how to heal without his help!

But I also think that we can anthropomorphize the cancer itself. That is Mom's enemy. If a lament begins with a complaint (or true lament) it often continues with a prayer to God for action. The doubts and anger and soul-searching, you see, do not preclude faith. Just the opposite! Doubt is not the opposite of faith (as many suppose); trusting in something other than God is the opposite of faith. True prayer is simple, true-to-life asking and begging. (True prayer is not all this meditative nonsense that passes for prayer these days.) A simple "Dear God, help!" is more truly heard by God than all the "babbling and bellowing" (Luther's description) that passes for prayer in many churches. Look how simple the prayer is here in verse 1: "Answer me!" (Now there's a believer with chutzpah!); "If you don't, I will die." (Don't think that Mother and I can't pray that!) And finally, "Then my enemies will win." That is: Who is God here: cancer or the creator of heaven and earth? That's why we finally pray, "Your kingdom come." We pray for God to act on earth as in heaven, to bring heaven down to earth, to bring in the resurrection when death and sickness shall be no more, and God will wipe away every tear from our eyes.

Laments most often end with faith (trust) and praise. In fact, psalms of trust (like Psalm 23 or 27) and psalms of praise (Psalm 150 etc.) may be reflections of these final parts of laments. Only Psalm 88 sticks with lament and prayer. Here in Psalm 13 the trust is simple and to the point. What sustains us in the midst of our sorrow? God's *hesed*, translated in the King James Version as "mercy" or here in the NRSV as "steadfast love" (v. 5). We simply have God's promise to sustain us—nothing more or less. The praise (vv. 5b–6) is in the future. The psalms, you see, are not Pollyannaish—pretending that all the feelings of sorrow and questioning disappear if one screws up enough energy really to trust God. This is an "up-the-ladder" religion for you—typical for people who talk about having more (or less) faith—"if only I were stronger, etc., then God would have listened." That's all demonic. Instead, the psalmist's faith keeps things in the future.

When God answers our prayer, shows himself to us, and reveals his steadfast love, then we will rejoice in that salvation and sing because of the Lord's bounty. Sometimes that happens even in the midst of sorrow. Your mother and I are often amazed and gladdened at the care that has surrounded us, how we have rediscovered our love for each other (even when we fight) and the love of others for us. That, too, is the Lord's bounty. And if we refrain from speculating about the future but concentrate on today's daily bread, it truly shows God's steadfast love.

Prayer: Dear God, how long? Answer us. Reveal your steadfast love so that we may again and again rejoice in Christ our Lord. Amen.

Psalm 23

From Martin Luther's *Summaries of the Psalms*

The Twenty-Third Psalm is a psalm of thanksgiving. In it a Christian heart praises and thanks God that God loves such a heart, holds it in the right path and comforts and protects it in all its needs through his holy Word. And the psalmist compares himself to a sheep, which a true shepherd pastures well in fresh grass and by cool water. Likewise, the psalmist also sets up table, cup, and oil as a comparison for the Old Testament and its worship of God. And all of these things point to God's word, as with rod, staff, grass, water, and the right way. This psalm belongs to the third commandment and the second petition.[7]

Meditation: "Trusting God in the Valley"

Emily, this is one of Mom's favorites, along with Psalm 116. We like it best in the old translation—I suppose most folk do. As a pastor, I had to recite it at most funerals, so I have become a little jaded. For me to see what it means to Mom helps remind me just how comforting it is. Psalms of lament often have four parts: cry to God, description of the predicament, trust in God, and praise for God's answer. A psalm of trust, like Psalm 23, in some ways is simply the third part of a lament. It is such a powerful testimony of faith that it can stand alone (without the other three parts), as it does here and elsewhere. (Psalm 27 is another psalm of trust.) The same is true for some psalms of praise.

"The Lord is my shepherd, I shall not be in want." (I'm using the version in *Lutheran Book of Worship* throughout.) The Israelites called their kings shepherd (see Ezekiel 34), so this beginning is a bit subversive. Unlike other nations in the Near East, where the king was often deified or seen as a projection of the gods (also true of Egypt's pharaohs, etc.), the Hebrews knew that there was only one true shepherd: the Lord (= Yahweh).

7. WA 38:25, 13–21.

That statement of faith distinguishes the Bible's religion from all the others.

> He makes me lie down in green pastures
>   and leads me beside still waters.
> He revives my soul
>   and guides me along right pathways
> for his name's sake. (vv. 2–3)

God is like an actual shepherd. We once had a woman come to Cross Lutheran Church with a lamb. She mentioned how sheep cannot drink from rivers with moving water but only from pools—still water. The green pastures are good food. The word "soul" here means "whole person." The revival spoken of is a result of receiving food and drink. The final part, "guidance along right pathways," is in the old translation, "paths of righteousness." The Hebrew word *tsedeq*, righteous, is a powerful one. Taking the wrong paths can mean getting lost or falling off a cliff. And "for his name's sake" points to God's honor. Indeed, our righteousness is not a matter of our finding our own path but in God leading us and guiding us and proclaiming us righteous—as a matter of *his* pride, *his* name, and *his* reputation.

> Though I walk through the valley of the shadow of death,
>   I shall fear no evil;
> for you are with me;
>   your rod and your staff,
>   they comfort me.
> You spread a table before me
>   in the presence of those who trouble me;
> you have anointed my head with oil,
>   and my cup is running over. (vv. 4–5)

There is a change here from the third person ("the Lord") to the second-person singular. It is as if the psalmist's faith bubbles over and he cannot contain himself but must address God directly. This "valley of the shadow of death" is better understood as "the darkest valley" or "a valley dark as death." But for countless centuries believers have heard these words and applied them not just to frightening places in the wilderness (especially for a sheep) but to death itself. There come these chilling breezes, and the fear of separation, loss, grief, sorrow, and death itself can overwhelm us. In those moments, there is this psalm—though I walk through *that* valley, "you are with me." My favorite name for God (and Jesus in Matthew 1): Emmanuel—God *with* us. In those moments of darkness—when we cannot see God, or ourselves, or one another—we can only feel God's correcting, caressing touch: the waters of baptism splashing over our brow, the taste of bread and wine at the Lord's Supper, the comforting voice of the Shepherd in the dark.

We eat at peace—even in the midst of enemies. That is the amazing thing about faith. It is not Pollyannaish, pretending things are going well when they really aren't. It is honest and truthful. Here are the problems; here is the evil around us. God allows us to eat and live in the midst of enemies—even cancer. The anointing is such a special thing for Israel. Kings, priests, and prophets are anointed. We call Jesus "Christ," which means messiah, which itself means "Anointed One." He is our prophet, priest, and king—and he, too, prays this prayer in faith, and we do the same through him. For our baptism (like his!) is our anointing—not just the cross traced in oil on our foreheads (as was the tradition already in the earliest church) but also the water itself and the gift of the Holy Spirit. And our cup is running over with blessings.

As you know, yesterday Lance Armstrong won the Tour de France for the second time running. He is a cancer survivor. Yesterday in the *Philadelphia Inquirer*, the sports columnist Bill Lyon wrote about Armstrong's fight with cancer and about one of the things he said in his autobiography. "Good, strong people get cancer, and they do all the right things to beat it, and they still die. So why don't we just stop and lie down? Because people with cancer live, too, and in the most remarkable ways."[8] A feast in the presence of enemies; life in the midst of death! It is amazing how the relation between Barbara and myself (and the rest of my family too) has been strengthened.

8. Bill Lyon, "Armstrong's Return to Cycling's Summit Is Stuff of Legends," Philadelphia Inquirer, July 2, 2000.

Surely [your] goodness and mercy shall follow me
   all the days of my life,
and I will dwell in the house of the Lord forever. (v. 6)

The word *your* is not in the text and shouldn't be, so I put it in brackets. Here the psalmist looks up again and realizes that he is talking to others, so God is now in the third person. That goodness and mercy follow us around is such an interesting image! In a way every believer, from the shepherd-king David to the present, looks to dwell in God's house. The word that is most encouraging is "forever." Even though the Hebrews didn't have much of a concept of heaven or life after death or even resurrection (unlike the New Testament), they fill their psalms of trust with the word "forever" (*ha 'ôlām*). It is as if their faith were stretching beyond what they knew and believed, to encompass everything—life, death, even time—in God's promised blessing. There is no end to God's promise. He holds us in life and in death; in this world and the next. No wonder this is such a comforting psalm!

Prayer: Good Shepherd, do not let us stray from you. Amen.

Psalm 46

Martin Luther's "A Mighty Fortress Is Our God" (based on Psalm 46)[9]

A mighty fortress is our God,
a sword and shield victorious;
he breaks the cruel oppressor's rod
and wins salvation glorious
The old evil foe,
sworn to work us woe,
with dread craft and might
he arms himself to fight.
On earth he has no equal.

---

9. *Evangelical Lutheran Worship* (Minneapolis: Augsburg Fortress, 2006), no. 503.

No strength of ours can match his might!
We would be lost, rejected.
But now a champion comes to fight,
whom God himself elected.
Ask who this may be:
Lord of hosts is he!
Christ Jesus our Lord,
God's only Son, adored.
He holds the field victorious.

Though hordes of devils fill the land
all threatening to devour us,
we tremble not, unmoved we stand;
they cannot overpow'r us.
This world's prince may rage,
in fierce war engage.
He is doomed to fail;
God's judgment must prevail!
One little word subdues him.

God's Word forever shall abide,
no thanks to foes, who fear it;
for God himself fights by our side
with weapons of the Spirit.
If they take our house,
goods, fame, child, or spouse,
wrench our life away,
they cannot win the day.
The kingdom's ours forever.

From Martin Luther's *Summaries of the Psalms*

Psalm 46 is a psalm of thanksgiving. It was sung by the people of
Israel for God's wondrous deeds, at the time when he protected
and defended the city of Jerusalem, which was his dwelling
place, against the raging and ranting of all kings and nations
and when he preserved its peace against all wars and weapons.
And, in the manner of Scripture, it calls the city's essence a small
fount, a little rivulet, that shall not dry up over against the great
bodies of water, seas, and oceans of the nations (that is, the great
kingdoms, principalities, and powers), that must dry up and pass

away. We, however, sing this psalm to praise God: that he is with us, that he preserves his word and Christianity miraculously against the gates of hell, against the raging of all devils, wretched spirits, the world, the flesh, sins, death, and the like. This little fountain of ours remains a living spring, since those swamps, deep pools, and cisterns become rotten and smelly and must dry up.[10]

Meditation: "Reformation by God's Active Voice Alone"

This psalm was one of Luther's favorite, and he used it to write "A Mighty Fortress Is Our God," a sure defense and weapon. His hymn is more an interpretation than a literal rendering of the psalm. But in that way he may be closer to the truth of the psalm than a mere translation would be. God is our refuge and strength, our help in trouble. This is a psalm of trust, and it says right up front who it is that we trust by describing what God does. Too many people want to worship God for what God is: holy, righteous, all-powerful, and so on. But true faith rests secure in what God does. This becomes evident in verses 2–3. We will not fear no matter what happens—even if, as Luther wrote in verse 3 of his hymn (the way I memorized it years ago), "devils all the world should fill, / all threatening to devour us, we tremble not, we fear no ill, / they cannot overpower us." Not bad. Though cancer, death, Alzheimer's, and so on may fill the world, we still have (or, better, are held by) God.

The psalmist then describes a city with God in its midst. He probably has Jerusalem in mind. In fact, some scholars think this psalm was written shortly after the Assyrian leader Sennacherib had besieged Jerusalem, only suddenly to decamp and return to Assyria. No wonder the psalmist seems so assured. "God is in the midst . . . It shall not be moved" (v. 5). In verses 6 and 8, the psalmist describes God as powerful over evil. God's voice sounds forth and the earth melts! Interspersed in verse 7 and again in verse 11 is a refrain (some think it belongs after v. 3 as well).

10. WA 38:35, 7–19.

The Lord of hosts is with us;
the God of Jacob is our refuge.

Luther ascribes this to Christ. He is the *rechter Mann* (right man), that is, champion of the joust fighting on behalf of another, who defeats our worst enemy, the devil (along with all the lesser enemies out there).

Not only does the Lord devastate the earth (v. 8), but he also, by the same token, brings war to an end (apparently through his power). He quiets them with a single command, a single word. "Be still, and know that I am God" (v. 10). That's the whole point. We live and cling to God's Word alone, and thus all of our activity must cease in the presence of God's "little word," as Luther calls it in his hymn. "Be still!" Again, like so many other psalms, this one, too, calls us away from works to faith alone.

Prayer: Dear God, you know our weakness. Be our strength in Jesus's name. Amen.

Psalm 119(:1–8)

From Martin Luther's Preface to His German Works (1539)[11]

I want to point out to you a correct way of studying theology, for I have had practice in that. If you keep to it, you will become so learned that you yourself could (if it were necessary) write books just as good as those of the fathers and councils, even as I (in God) dare to presume and boast, without arrogance and lying, that in the matter of writing books I do not stand much behind some of the fathers. Of my life I can by no means make the same boast. This is the way taught by holy King David (and doubtlessly used also by all the patriarchs and prophets) in the one hundred nineteenth psalm. There you will find three rules, amply presented throughout the whole psalm. They are *oratio*, *meditatio*, *tentatio*.[12]

---

11. AL 4:482–88 (WA 50:657–60), leaving out his description of the early phases of the Reformation.

12. Literally: prayer, meditation, temptation. By using the Latin words in an otherwise German text, Luther is making a connection to and correction of the tra-

Oratio [prayer]. Firstly, you should know that the Holy Scriptures constitute a book that turns the wisdom of all other books into foolishness, because not one teaches about eternal life except this one alone. Therefore you should straightway despair of your reason and understanding. With them you will not attain eternal life, but, on the contrary, your presumptuousness will plunge you and others with you out of heaven (as happened to Lucifer) into the abyss of hell. But kneel down in your little room [Matt 6:6] and pray to God with real humility and earnestness, that he through his dear Son may give you his Holy Spirit, who will enlighten you, lead you, and give you understanding.

Thus you see how David keeps praying in the abovementioned psalm, "Teach me, Lord, instruct me, lead me, show me," and many more words like these.[13] Although he well knew and daily heard and read the text of Moses and other books besides, still he wants to lay hold of the real teacher of the Scriptures himself, so that he may not seize upon them pell-mell with his reason and become his own teacher. For such practice gives rise to factious spirits who allow themselves to nurture the delusion that the Scriptures are subject to them and can be easily grasped with their reason, as if they were *Markolf*, or *Aesop's Fables*, for which no Holy Spirit and no prayers are needed.[14]

Meditatio [meditation]. Secondly, you should meditate, that is, not only in your heart, but also externally, by actually repeating and comparing oral speech and literal words of the book, reading and rereading them with diligent attention and reflection, so that you may see what the Holy Spirit means by them. And take care that you do not grow weary or think that you have done

---

ditional monastic practice of *lectio divina*, i.e., "*lectio, meditatio, oratio,* and finally *contemplatio* (reading, meditating, prayer, and contemplation). By putting prayer first (in a reflection of how foolish Scripture sounds to human reason) and, more importantly, by replacing contemplation with *tentatio* (by which Luther means not simply temptations of the flesh but *Anfechtung,* the attacks and assaults of the devil, the world, and the flesh), he presents an evangelical way of reading Scripture that prevents the exegete from gaining control over the text.

13. E.g., Ps 119:12, 26, 33, 35, 64, 108, 124, 135.

14. *Markolf* refers to a set of medieval tales about a dialogue between King Solomon and the trickster Markolf, who often outwits the king with his foolishness. Luther had high regard for Aesop and even began editing the fables in 1530 while at the Coburg Castle.

enough when you have read, heard, and spoken them once or twice, and that you then have complete understanding. You will never be a particularly good theologian if you do that, for you will be like untimely fruit which falls to the ground before it is half ripe.

Thus you see in this same psalm how David constantly boasts that he will talk, meditate, speak, sing, hear, read, by day and night and always about nothing except God's word and commandments. For God will not give you his Spirit without the external word; so take your cue from that. His command to write, preach, read, hear, sing, speak, etc. outwardly was not given in vain.

Tentatio [assault]. Thirdly, there is *tentatio*, *Anfechtung* [assault or attack]. This is the touchstone that teaches you not only to know and understand, but also to experience how right, how true, how sweet, how lovely, how mighty, how comforting God's word is, wisdom beyond all wisdom.

Thus you see how David, in the psalm mentioned, complains so often about all kinds of enemies, arrogant princes or tyrants, false spirits and factions, whom he must tolerate because he meditates, that is, because he is occupied with God's word (as has been said) in all manner of ways.[15] For as soon as God's word takes root and grows in you, the devil will harry you, and will make a real doctor [teacher] of you, and by his assaults will teach you to seek and love God's word. I myself (if you will permit me, mere mouse droppings, to be mingled with the pepper) am deeply indebted to my papists that through the devil's raging they have beaten, oppressed, and distressed me so much. That is to say, they have made a fairly good theologian of me, which I would not have become otherwise. And I heartily grant them what they have won in return for making this of me, honor, victory, and triumph, for that's the way they wanted it.

There now, with that you have David's rules. If you study hard in accord with his example, then you will also sing and boast with him in the psalm [119:72], "The law of your mouth is better to me than thousands of gold and silver pieces." Also

15. E.g., Ps 119:22–23, 51, 61, 69–71, 78, 84–87, 95, 110, 115, 134, 141, 143, 150, 153, 157, 161.

[119:98–100], "Your commandment makes me wiser than my enemies, for it is ever with me. I have more understanding than all my teachers, for your testimonies are my meditation. I understand more than the aged, for I keep your precepts. . . ." And it will be your experience that the books of the fathers will taste stale and putrid to you in comparison. You will not only despise the books written by adversaries, but the longer you write and teach the less you will be pleased with yourself. When you have reached this point, then do not be afraid to hope that you have begun to become a real theologian, who can teach not only the young and imperfect Christians, but also the maturing and perfect ones. For indeed, Christ's church has all kinds of Christians in it who are young, old, weak, sick, healthy, strong, energetic, lazy, simple, wise, etc.

If, however, you feel and are inclined to think you have made it, flattering yourself with your own little books, teaching, or writing, because you have done it beautifully and preached excellently; if you are highly pleased when someone praises you in the presence of others; if you perhaps look for praise and would sulk or quit what you are doing if you did not get it—if you are of that stripe, dear friend, then take yourself by the ears, and if you do this in the right way you will find a beautiful pair of big, long, shaggy donkey ears. Then do not spare any expense! Decorate them with golden bells, so that people will be able to hear you wherever you go, point their fingers at you, and say, "See, see! There goes that clever beast, who can write such exquisite books and preach so remarkably well." That very moment you will be blessed and blessed beyond measure in the kingdom of heaven—yes, in that heaven where hellfire is ready for the devil and his angels. To sum up: Let us be proud and seek honor in the places where we may. But in this Book the honor is God's alone, as it is said, "God opposes the proud, but gives grace to the humble" [1 Pet 5:5]; to whom be glory, world without end, Amen.

From Martin Luther's *Summaries of the Psalms*

Psalm 119 is a long psalm, which contains a boatload of prayer, comfort, teaching, and thanksgiving. It is, however, principally made to attract us to God's word, which it praises over and over and warns us about false teachers as well as about becoming weary with and despising it. For this reason, it is for the most part to be reckoned a psalm of comfort, since truly everything depends on having God's word pure and hearing it eagerly. From this then follows inevitably and powerfully praying, teaching, comforting, thanking, prophesying, serving God, suffering, and everything else that pleases God and makes the devil bitter. When a person despises God's word or has had enough of it, then the Word takes second place to everything else, and where it is not purely taught, then there may well be plenty of praying, teaching, comforting, thanking, serving God, suffering, and prophesying—but all completely false and for naught. For then everything serves the devil, who makes it all impure with his heresy.[16]

Meditation: "Walking and Praying by Faith Alone"

Psalm 119 is an acrostic psalm, with each of the eight verses starting with the successive letter of the Hebrew alphabet. This is the letter Aleph. It is a psalm of praise of God's Torah, or law. But here law is not understood simply as that which accuses us and shows our sin but as God's very voice. And the perspective from which the psalmist praises the Torah is that of pure faith, so that he is not looking at his sin but at the new heart and life given by faith alone. This truly is a paean to God's Word.

The first three verses announce that it is all about faith, not works or merits. It talks of the *halakah*—the way and the walk (v. 1). That arises out of faith. In order to be clear, verse 2 talks of "keeping" God's decrees and "seeking" him with the "whole heart." That's key: the whole heart means that it is a matter of

16. WA 38:57, 8–20.

faith. Verse 3 then adds that works follow (who *also* [in addition to or as a result of faith] do no wrong) but returns to the walk.

Next we hear a prayer (vv. 4–8) directed now to God, for from faith arises prayer. In fact, Emily, as I like to say, prayer is simply faith breathing. The psalmist begins with God's will and demand (v. 4) and then melts into faith (v. 5)—begging God that his "ways" and "keeping" may be steadfast and firm. What is that but faith? Trusting God to do the very thing God commands! As St. Augustine put it in his *Confessions*, "Give what you command, O Lord, and command whatever you want."

The last half of the prayer (vv. 6–8) describes to God the consequence of God's answering this prayer of faith—a prayer, by the way, that arises not out of our fullness but out of our emptiness. What are the consequences? No shame (v. 6; note, by the way, "eyes fixed on" is another picture for faith), praise (v. 7; note here the "upright heart" and "learn your righteous ordinances"—all matters of faith), observing the commandments (v. 8). The final verse returns to the cry of faith: "Do not utterly forsake me." Ah, there it is! That's where you and I live now, Emily, each day—crying to God out of faith alone: "Do not utterly forsake me." That one line summarizes ten months of our prayers. Oh, to have the faith to pray that prayer!

Prayer: Dear God, grant us faith; do not forsake us, through Christ our Lord. Amen.

Psalm 130

From Martin Luther's *Summaries of the Psalms*

Psalm 130 is prayer psalm, which arises out of true Davidic zeal and understanding. For he confesses that no one may be righteous in God's sight through his [or her] own works and righteousness but only through grace and forgiveness of sins that God has promised. He builds on such promise and word and comforts himself, and he admonishes all Israel that it should also do and learn that with God there is a throne of grace and redemption. And Israel must through him alone—and otherwise not at all—be free of all sins. That is, through forgiveness it becomes righteous and blessed (else it would not be grace). Otherwise he may well remain in the depths and never be able to stand before God at all. See? This is the true master and teacher of the Holy Scriptures. He understood what it means that the "seed of the woman is to tread upon the head of the serpent" (Gen 3:15). And, "through your seed shall all the people of earth be blessed" (Gen 22:18). Therefore, place both of these promises and prophecies about Christ into this verse: "He will redeem Israel from all his sins." The entire psalm stands on and goes forth from this verse.[17]

Meditation: "Crying from the Depths"

De profundis is the Latin title of this psalm. The monks (and even Luther) named the psalms according to the first words of the Latin version. "Out of the depths." This is one of the so-called penitential psalms, and Luther wrote one of his first hymns based on it. The translations in most hymnbooks leave much to be desired. This is the way the old translation (by Catherine Winkworth) went:

> Out of the depths I cry to Thee,
> Lord God, oh hear my prayer.
> Incline a gracious ear to me,
> And bid me not despair.
> If Thou rememberest each misdeed,
> If each should have its rightful meed,
> Lord, who shall stand before Thee?
>
> Lord, through Thy love alone we gain
> The pardon of our sin;
> The strictest life is but in vain,
> Our works can nothing win,
> That none should boast himself of aught,
> But own in fear Thy grace hath wrought
> What in him seemeth righteous.
>
> Wherefore my hope is in the Lord,
> My works I count but dust,

17. WA 38:60, 30–61, 14.

I build not there, but on His word,
And in His goodness trust.
Up to His care myself I yield,
He is my tower, my rock, my shield,
And for his help I tarry.

And though it tarry till the night
And round again to morn,
My heart shall ne'er mistrust Thy might,
Nor count itself forlorn.
Do thus, O ye of Israel's seed,
Ye of the Spirit born indeed;
Wait for your God's appearing.

Though great our sins and sore our wounds,
And deep and dark our fall,
His helping mercy hath no bounds,
His love surpasseth all.
Our truly loving Shepherd He,
Who shall at last set Israel free
From all their sin and sorrow.[18]

Luther has written both paraphrase and commentary on that hymn. Psalm 130 is a kind of lament over sins, but it also arises out of—you guessed it—faith alone. In verses 1–2 the psalmist cries to God in his need. "Out of the depths." Not only of sin, but also fears, anxieties, sorrow, loneliness, pain, oppression, and sadness. If God does not hear our complaints, all is lost. Verses 3–4 say we can cry to God because God will not let anything—even sin—stand between him and us. If he kept a record, we'd all be in a heap of trouble! But—amazing grace—there is forgiveness with him. Now this forgiveness does not lead to treating God like a dupe ("Oh, I'll just go and sin, because God forgives me"), but forgiveness is so unexpected, so contrary to what we would imagine from the God who rules heaven and earth, that we revere (or, in the old, better translation, fear) him. Fear, because we deserve punishment; fear, because God acts in a way contrary to all expectation. God can do anything, but God has chosen to forgive us our sins! *Mirabile!*

18. Catherine Winkworth, *Lyra Germanica: Hymns for the Sundays and Chief Festivals of the Christian Year* (New York: Delisser & Procter, 1859), 65–66.

The result of God's forgiveness—faith (which is the same as hope and expectation)—comes in verses 5–6. Everything depends on God, so we wait for God to act. The sooner the better! This dependence is true not only of forgiveness but also of healing and, finally, resurrection. "Your kingdom come" (and soon)! The basis of our faith and hope (vv. 7–8) is God's *ḥesed* (steadfast love) and redemption. That's why Luther keeps saying, "Not by my merit!" And he's right; that's what this psalm is all about:

O Israel, hope in the Lord!
  For with the Lord there is steadfast love,
  and with him is great power to redeem.

What else do we have, Emily? Where else can we turn but to God, who loved us to death—his own death on the cross?

Prayer: Out of the depths we cry to you, O Lord. Lord, hear our voice! Let your ears be attentive to the voice of our supplications, through Christ our Lord. Amen.

Psalm 139

From Martin Luther's *Summaries of the Psalms*

Psalm 139 is a psalm of thanksgiving in which [the psalmist] praises God because God has so wonderfully protected him and continues to rule him in all his thoughts, words, and deeds, whether standing, walking, sleeping, or waking. Indeed, even in his mother's womb, before he was created, God was with him [and knew] how he would grow up and how long he would live. It was as if he said, "It is not a part of human artifice or power [to determine] how he lives, acts, speaks, or thinks, where and when he does these things, whither he comes or goes. Instead, it is all completely and purely God's work and skill."

For what do the completely godless do who do not believe this except to desire to become righteous on their own using their disgusting works? They want to have done what they do and want to receive merit, praise, and honor from God, when in fact they have not manufactured a single word out of themselves and they cannot construct a single thought from their own powers. They do not even know what they are doing, how they were created, how they live, speak, and think.

So, then, everything that we are and do is God's work and skill. How human beings arrogate to themselves works of supererogation: that make themselves righteous, that vaunt their free will, and that will free them from sin and death, and so on. Such people cannot speak rightly about God and his works. Protect me, Lord from them, prove me, and cleanse my heart, so that I remain in the right path that will last eternally.[19]

Meditation: "God Really Cares for Us"

This psalm is your Grandma Wengert's favorite. It is a beautiful expression of God's care for us. In the first six verses, the psalmist expresses God's complete knowledge of us and is overwhelmed (in v. 6). No matter what we say or think or do, God knows us front, back, and center (v. 5). In verses 7–12, the psalmist considers God's unfailing presence with us. No matter where we go, God is there. Even in the darkness, Emily, God is there with us.

Then, in verses 13–18 (every six verses there's a new theme), the psalmist turns to our creation. A friend of mine once said that he pictured God as a little woman, sitting all scrunched up in a mother's womb, knitting furiously (v. 13). I can still remember when you were first born, marveling over your tiny fingers and—most amazing of all—fingerprints! Such a miracle! Verse 18 then summarizes the psalmist's wonder.

The last six verses are something of a disappointment—at first glance. Here come those enemies again. Why can't the psalmist just content himself with sweetness and light? The answer comes in the nature of true faith. It is not simply wonder at God's knowledge, presence, and creative power but an intense trust in God that will broach no competition. Here is this wonderful God, and yet there are those who want only evil and have nothing good to say about God ("those who speak of you maliciously, and lift themselves up against you for evil," v. 20). We

19. WA 38:64, 3–22.

can even go a step further than the psalmist and pray that the evil, doubts, fears, and despair that we encounter *in ourselves* be "killed," extinguished. Here, finally, the psalmist is actually praying for faith, for more and more trust in God. In the end, to hate evil is to rely solely on the love and mercy of God alone and, as the psalmist says at the end, to be purged of all wickedness. That last verse puts things in a different perspective, where the psalmist asks God to examine him and lead him in the way everlasting. One can almost imagine poor, persecuted Jeremiah praying this psalm. Don't let any evil—even cancer—interfere with my relation to you, O God!

Prayer: Dear God, you know us, you are with us, and you created us. So, please, lead us to everlasting life in Christ. Amen.[20]

Psalm 145

From Martin Luther's *Summaries of the Psalms*

Psalm 145 is a psalm of thanksgiving for Christ's kingdom that was coming in the future. And it greatly emphasizes [*treibet*] this work: praising God and exulting in God's power and kingdom. For Christ's kingdom and power are hidden under the cross. Were a person not to vaunt this through preaching, teaching, and confessing, who could possibly imagine anything about it—to say nothing of knowing it for certain? But his power and kingdom are of this kind: that he lifts up the fallen, receives the suffering, makes the sinner righteous and the dead alive. Indeed, he is the one who nourishes all, who hears the cries of his saints, does what they desire, protects them, and the like.[21]

Meditation: "Praise No Matter What!"

This psalm is a song of praise, perhaps an odd psalm to read in our situation with Mom dying. As Luther said, "When a sad man

20. This psalm was prayed by our pastor at Barbara's bedside only a few minutes before she died.
21. WA 38:67, 4–12.

laughs or a happy man cries, they do not do so from the heart." But, in fact, this psalm puts life in its proper perspective. It is about living in and under the sovereign God. The first seven verses are simply an invitation to praise based on God's mighty works. The psalmist is overwhelmed by all that God has done. And it *is* true. To think that I did not know whether we would all live to see this day. I was worried whether Mom would see David in his high school play next week! It shows how little faith I had or, rather, how little I know of the future. Best to leave such matters in God's hands and—as always—concentrate on the particular, real blessings of this day.

"Take no thought for the morrow!" Ah, yes, Lord, I know that, but it takes so much more faith than I have. What is God's work that so leads the psalmist to praise? Verses 8–9 form the heart of this psalm. The psalmist quotes Exodus 34:6, where God reveals himself to Moses and the people of Israel with these very words:

The Lord is gracious and merciful,
    slow to anger and abounding in steadfast love. (Ps 145:8)

There it is! Even the sorrowful can genuinely praise the God who *at heart* is merciful, good, compassionate. And then the psalmist goes back to praising (vv. 10–13a), convinced that not just "one generation . . . to another" (v. 4) but "all your works" will sing praise. Why? Because God's merciful, gracious, love-filled rule—which is his kingdom—is everlasting. It will even outlast death.

Verses 13b–16 give yet another glimpse into the heart of God and the scope of his works. First, he is "faithful in all his words," which means that we can rely on his promises, and "gracious in all his deeds," which means that he is filled with grace. Now look at verse 14. There is where we come in when we are down—grieving over heaven knows what. This is the kind of God we have:

The Lord upholds all who are falling,
    and raises up all who are bowed down.

Thank heavens! There is hope in him. Then in verses 15–16 there is one of our table blessings—it is the same as Psalm 104:27. God's grace is proved each time we use this "grace," that is, every time we eat.

Verses 17–19 give another hint of God's works: he answers our prayers. "He also hears their cry, and saves them" (v. 19). Did I know that he would so strengthen my faith, cause me to be so strong with your mother? Had I any idea how much he would carry us on through the prayers of others? Or how courageous your mother would be? No! And yet, God heard my cry (probably just a simple, "Help!") and answered it far beyond my wildest dreams and hopes. Of course, no psalm would be complete without the wicked. Why is that? Because the psalmists are realists (that is, believers), not idealists (dreamers). They know how things really are, and they tell it like it is. "All the wicked he will destroy" (v. 20). Thank God! It is not just that God does good things but can't handle evil. God is truly sovereign, and because he is a good ruler, he will also eradicate all wickedness and evils around us and in us. He will even eliminate cancer one day! So, you see, even we can say (v. 21):

> My mouth will speak the praise of the Lord,
>   and all flesh will bless his name forever and ever.

Prayer: Open your hand, O Lord, and satisfy the desire of all who trust in you through Christ our Lord. Amen.

Appendix: Philip Melanchthon on the Word *Justification* in 1532

In his 1532 *Commentaries on Romans*, for the first time Philip Melanchthon pointed out that Paul's use of the word *justification* in Romans was a Hebraism. This linguistic insight supported his insistence in the Apology of the Augsburg Confession (1531) that the justification of the sinner did not occur through an indwelling of Christ's essential righteousness nor did God declare a person righteous based on his or her past, present, or future righteous actions. Instead God's declaration of forgiveness justified the sinner. Prior or future works of righteousness did not contribute to this "imputed" righteousness. In 1532, he places this discussion in the *argumentum* of Romans, in a special section titled "Prolegomena on Justification."[1] It begins:

> So that we may prepare the reader to understand the case that Paul is making, let us draw together the sum of the matter as one does in organizing an academic structure [*methodus*]. To be sure, the letter of Paul itself expounds matters in a reasonable order and clearly in a methodical [*methodice*] way. And because it also hands on the principal and proper locus of Christian teaching it must be judged as if [providing] a kind of structure [*methodus*] for the entire Scripture.[2]

---

1. Philip Melanchthon, *Commentarii in Epistolam Pauli ad Romanos* (Wittenberg: Klug, 1532), 1 vii^v. For the modern edition of this text, see MSA 5:33.
2. Melanchthon, *Commentarii*, 1 vii^v–viii^r (MSA 5:33).

(Melanchthon examines several aspects of justification, including the topics of sin, law, faith, and gospel, but he also defines the words "justification" and "righteous" in Pauline usage.)

Thus, Paul teaches about justification as follows. The Gospel preaches repentance and "proves [the world wrong] about sin" [John 16:8] and offers forgiveness of sins, justification, and eternal life to all—not on account of our worthiness or our works or our disposition or virtues but through mercy on account of Christ, as long as they believe this, namely that God is certainly well-disposed to them on account of Christ. He teaches this when he says (Rom. 3:28), "We hold that a person is justified by faith apart from works prescribed by the law." Or, again (Rom. 10:10), "It is believed in the heart for righteousness." And they [i.e., the Reformers] say it with other words: "By faith alone a person is justified." Using statements of this kind, this type of discourse ought to be understood.

To be justified properly means to be reputed righteous, that is, to be reputed accepted. Thus it may be understood in relation [relative],[3] since it is practiced in a court [of law] according to Hebraic custom, that "to be justified" stands for "to be pronounced righteous," as when someone says that the Roman people justified Scipio,[4] who was accused by the tribune of the people.[5] That is, the people pronounced him righteous, absolved, and approved him.

---

3. In Latin syntax, there are two ways to understand a term: *proprie* (properly), that is, according to its basic (in this case, philosophical) meaning, or *relative* (in relation or relatively), in its specific context. (English still uses the term *relative pronoun*, through which a pronoun is related [by ownership] to a noun.) Thus, for Melanchthon justification cannot be understood strictly speaking (as defined by Aristotle and Cicero) as "giving to each his [or her] own" but only relatively speaking, that is, in relation to God's mercy in Christ and thus as God's acceptance and declaration that the sinner is righteous.

4. Scipio, the hero of the Punic Wars, had been caught embezzling money from the common funds in Rome. When called to make an account of himself before the tribunes, the Roman people surrounded him on his way to court, shouting that every mother in Rome should give birth to such a child as Scipio. Scipio, who was clearly guilty of what was then a capital crime, was "pronounced" righteous by the crowd. For more information about this story and its role in Melanchthon's thought, see Timothy J. Wengert, *Defending Faith: Lutheran Responses to Andreas Osiander's Doctrine of Justification* (Tübingen: Mohr Siebeck, 2012), 338–43.

5. The *Tribuni plebis*, "whose office it was to defend the rights and interests of the Roman plebeians against the encroachments of the patricians." See Charles T. Lewis and Charles Short, *A Latin Dictionary* (New York: Harper; Oxford: Oxford University Press, 1879), *ad loc.*

Although, to be sure, it is necessary for new impulses to exist in those who are reconciled, nevertheless to be justified, properly speaking [*proprie*], does not mean to have new virtues but may be understood relationally [*relative*] about God's will—because of which [a person] is approved or accepted by God.

"Righteous" in relational terms [*relative*] means accepted by God. Righteousness of the law is the obedience of our will to the law of God, namely, our virtues and actions, what philosophers call universal righteousness. But the imputation of righteousness, likewise the righteousness of God in these discussions of Paul and often elsewhere in Scripture, means acceptance relationally [*relative*], by which we are even accepted by God gratis, not on account of our virtues, which are not worthy for our being pronounced righteous nor can they stand over against God's judgment.[6]

6. Melanchthon, *Commentarii*, 2 iii^v–iv^r (MSA 5:38–40).

Bibliography

PRIMARY SOURCES

Augustine. *On Christian Doctrine.* Translated by D. W. Robertson. Indianapolis: Liberal Arts Press, 1958.

———. *On the Spirit and the Letter.* In *A Select Library of Nicene and Post-Nicene Fathers of the Christian Church,* edited by Philip Schaff, series 1, 5:83–114. 1886–1889. Reprint, Grand Rapids: Eerdmans, 1974.

———. *A Select Library of Nicene and Post-Nicene Fathers of the Christian Church.* Vol. 8, *Expositions on the Book of Psalms.* Edited by Philip Schaff. 1886–1889. Reprint, Grand Rapids: Eerdmans, 1974.

The Book of Concord. Edited by Robert Kolb and Timothy J. Wengert. Minneapolis: Fortress Press, 2000.

Bugenhagen, Johannes. *Conciliata ex Evangelistis historia passi Christi & glorificati, cum annotationibus.* In *Annotationes . . . iam emissae in Deuteronomium, in Samuelem prophetam, id est, duos libros Regum.* Basel: Petri, 1524.

Calvin, John. *Ioannis Calvini Opera Quae Supersunt Omnia.* 59 vols. Edited by Wilhelm Baum, Eduard Cunitz, and Eduard Reuss. Braunschweig, Leipzig, and Zurich, 1834–1900.

———. *Institutes of the Christian Religion.* Edited by John T. McNeill. Translated by Ford Lewis Battles. 2 vols. Philadelphia: Westminster, 1960.

Dietrich, Veit. *Summaria über die gantze Bibel.* Nuremberg: Vom Berg & Newber, 1545.

Erasmus of Rotterdam. *Ciceronianus*. In *Ausgewählte Schriften*, edited by Werner Welzig, 7:1–355. Darmstadt: Wissenschaftliche Buchgesellschaft, 1968–1972.

Evangelical Lutheran Worship. Minneapolis: Augsburg Fortress Press, 2006.

Grimm, Jacob, and Wilhelm Grimm et al., eds. *Deutsches Wörterbuch*. 16 vols. in 32 sections. Leipzig, 1854–1961. https://tinyurl.com/y9gglxap.

Kolb, Robert, et al., eds. *Sources and Contexts of the Book of Concord*. Minneapolis: Fortress Press, 2001.

Lefèvre d'Étaples, Jacques. *Qvincvplex Psalterium, Gallicum, Romanum, Hebraicum, Vetus, Conciliatum*. Paris: H. Stephan, 1509.

Luther, Martin. *Luthers Werke: Kritische Gesamtausgabe: Bibel*. 12 vols. Weimar: H. Böhlau, 1906–1961.

———. *Luthers Werke: Kritische Gesamtausgabe: Briefwechsel*, 18 vols. Weimar: H. Böhlau, 1930–1985.

———. *Luthers Werke: Kritische Gesamtausgabe* [*Schriften*]. 65 vols. Weimar: H. Böhlau, 1883–1993.

———. *Luther's Works* [American edition]. Edited by Jaroslav Pelikan et al. 82 vols. planned. Philadelphia: Fortress Press; St. Louis: Concordia, 1955–1986; 2009–.

———. *The Annotated Luther*. Edited by Hans Hillerbrand et al. 6 vols. Minneapolis: Fortress Press, 2015–2017.

Major, Georg. *De Origine et autoritate uerbi Dei, & quae Pontificum, Patrum & Conciliorum sit autoritas, admonitio hoc tempore, quo de Concilio congregando agitur, ualde necessaria. Additus est catalogus Doctorum Ecclesiae Dei, a mundi initio, usque ad haec tempora*. Wittenberg: J. Lufft, 1550.

Mathesius, Johann. *Ausgewählte Werke*. Vol. 3, *Luthers Leben in Predigten*. Edited by Georg Loesche. Prague: Calve, 1906.

Melanchthon, Philip. *Commentarii in Epistolam Pauli ad Romanos*. Wittenberg: Klug, 1532.

———. *Commonplaces: Loci Communes 1521*. Translated by Christian Preus. St. Louis: Concordia, 2014.

———. *Corpus Reformatorum: Philippi Melanthonis opera quae supersunt omnia*. Edited by Karl Bretschneider and Heinrich Bindseil. 28 vols. Halle: A. Schwetschke & Sons, 1834–1860.

———. *Melanchthons Werke* [Studienausgabe]. Edited by Robert Stupperich. 7 vols. Gütersloh: Bertelsmann, 1951–1975.

Mörlin, Joachim. *Historia Welcher gestalt sich die Osiandrische schwermerey im lande zu Preussen erhaben, vnd wie dieselbige verhandelt ist, mit allen actis beschrieben.* Magdeburg: Michael Lotter, 1554.

Nicholas of Lyra. *Biblia cum Postilla litteralis.* 4 vols. Lyon, ca. 1485.

Origen of Alexandria. *On First Principles* [*De principiis*]. Translated by G. W. Butterworth. Gloucester, MA: Peter Smith, 1973.

Winkworth, Catherine. *Lyra Germanica: Hymns for the Sundays and Chief Festivals of the Christian Year.* New York: Delisser & Procter, 1859.

SECONDARY SOURCES

Bayer, Oswald. *Theology the Lutheran Way.* Edited and translated by Jeffrey G. Silcock and Mark C. Mattes. Grand Rapids: Eerdmans, 2007.

Brecht, Martin. *Martin Luther: His Road to Reformation, 1483–1521.* Translated by James L. Schaaf. Philadelphia: Fortress Press, 1985.

Childs, Brevard. *Biblical Theology in Crisis.* Philadelphia: Westminster, 1970.

Dieter, Theodor. *Der junge Luther und Aristoteles: Eine historisch-systematische Untersuchung zum Verhältnis von Theologie und Philosophie.* Berlin: De Gruyter, 2001.

Dingel, Irene, ed. *Justus Jonas (1493–1555) und seine Bedeutung für die Wittenberger Reformation.* Leipzig: Evangelische Verlagsanstalt, 2009.

Ebeling, Gerhard. "The Beginnings of Luther's Hermeneutics." *Lutheran Quarterly* 7 (1993): 129–58, 315–38, 451–68.

———. *Evangelische Evangeliumauslegung: Eine Untersuchung zu Luthers Hermeneutik.* Munich: Kaiser, 1942.

———. "Kirchengeschichte als Geschichte der Auslegung der Heiligen Schrift." In *Wort Gottes und Tradition,* 9–27 Göttingen: Vandenhoeck & Ruprecht, 1964.

Engelbrecht, Edward A. *Friends of the Law: Luther's Use of the Law for the Christian Life.* St. Louis: Concordia, 2011.

Forde, Gerhard. *Theology Is for Proclamation*. Minneapolis: Fortress Press, 1990.

Fraenkel, Peter. *Testimonia Patrum: The Function of the Patristic Argument in the Theology of Philip Melanchthon*. Geneva: Droz, 1961.

Grane, Leif. *Modus loquendi theologicus: Luthers Kampf um die Erneuerung der Theologie (1515–1518)*. Leiden: Brill, 1975.

Hagen, Kenneth. *Luther's Approach to Scripture as Seen in His "Commentaries" on Galatians 1519–1538*. Tübingen: Mohr Siebeck, 1993.

Hamm, Berndt. *The Early Luther: Stages in a Reformation Reorientation*. Translated by Martin Lohrmann. Grand Rapids: Eerdmans, 2014.

Handy, Robert T. *A Christian America: Protestant Hopes and Historical Realities*. New York: Oxford University Press, 1971.

Heen, Erik. "A Lutheran Response to the New Perspective on Paul." *Lutheran Quarterly* 24 (2010): 263–91.

Hendrix, Scott. "Martin Luther's Reformation of Spirituality." *Lutheran Quarterly* 13 (1999): 249–70.

Johnson, Anna Marie. *Beyond Indulgences: Luther's Reform of Late Medieval Piety, 1518–1520*. Kirksville, MO: Truman State University Press, 2017.

Junghans, Helmar. *Der junge Luther und die Humanisten*. Weimar: Böhlau, 1984.

Kolb, Robert. *Bound Choice, Election, and Wittenberg Theological Method: From Martin Luther to the Formula of Concord*. Grand Rapids: Eerdmans, 2005.

———. *Martin Luther: Confessor of the Faith*. New York: Oxford University Press, 2009.

———. *Martin Luther and the Enduring Word of God: The Wittenberg School and Its Scripture-Centered Proclamation*. Grand Rapids: Baker Academic, 2016.

Kristeller, Paul Oskar. *Renaissance Thought and Its Sources*. Edited by Michael Mooney. New York: Columbia University Press, 1979.

Lathrop, Gordon, and Timothy J. Wengert. *Christian Assembly: Marks of the Church in a Pluralistic Age*. Minneapolis: Fortress Press, 2004.

Leppin, Volker, and Berndt Hamm, eds. *Gottes Nähe unmittelbar erfahren: Mystik im Mittelalter und bei Martin Luther*. Tübingen: Mohr Siebeck, 2007.

Muller, Richard. *The Unaccommodated Calvin: Studies in the Formation of a Theological Tradition*. New York: Oxford University Press, 2000.

Nestingen, James A. "Preaching Repentance." *Lutheran Quarterly* 3 (1989): 249–66.

O'Malley, John. "Luther the Preacher." In *The Martin Luther Quincentennial*, edited by Gerhard Dünnhaupt, 3–16. Detroit: Wayne State University Press, 1985.

Pizzolato, Luigi Franco. *La dottrina esegetica di sant Ambrogio*. Milan: Vita e Pensiero, 1978.

Preus, James Samuel. *From Shadow to Promise: Old Testament Interpretations from Augustine to the Young Luther*. Cambridge, MA: Harvard University Press, 1969.

Rad, Gerhard von. *Old Testament Theology*. Translated by D. M. G. Stalker. 2 vols. New York: Harper & Row, 1962–1965.

Räder, Siegfried. *Das Hebräische bei Luther untersucht bis zum Ende der ersten Psalmenvorlesung*. Tübingen: Mohr Siebeck, 1961.

———. *Die Benutzung des masoretischen Textes bei Luther in der Zeit zwischen der ersten und zweiten Psalmenvorlesung (1515–1518)*. Tübingen: Mohr Siebeck, 1966.

———. *Grammatica Theologica: Studien zu Luthers "Operationes in Psalmos."* Tübingen: Mohr Siebeck, 1977.

Schäfer, Rolf. "Melanchthon's Interpretation of Romans 5:15: His Departure from the Augustinian Concept of Grace Compared to Luther's." In *Philip Melanchthon (1497–1560) and the Commentary*, edited by Timothy J. Wengert and M. Patrick Graham, 79–104. Sheffield: Sheffield Academic, 1997.

Schmidt, Philipp. *Die Illustration der Lutherbibel 1522–1700: Ein Stück abendländische Kultur- und Kirchengeschichte mit Verzeichnissen der Bibeln, Bilder und Künstler*. Basel: Reinhardt, 1962.

Schwinge, Gerhard. *Melanchthon in der Druckgraphik: Eine Auswahl aus dem 17. bis 19. Jahrhundert*. Ubstadt-Weiher: Verlag Regionalkultur, 2000.

Smalley, Beryl. *The Study of the Bible in the Middle Ages*. Oxford: Blackwell, 1952.

Smart, James D. *The Strange Silence of the Bible in the Church: A Study in Hermeneutics*. Philadelphia: Westminster, 1970.

Springer, Carl P. E. *Cicero in Heaven: The Roman Rhetor and Luther's Reformation*. Leiden: Brill, 2018.

Steinmetz, David C. "The Superiority of Pre-Critical Exegesis." *Theology Today* 27 (1980): 27–38.

Stolt, Birgit. *"Laßt uns fröhlich springen!": Gefühlswelt und Gefühlsnavigierung in Luthers Reformationsarbeit*. Berlin: Weidler, 2012.

———. "Luther's Translation of the Bible." *Lutheran Quarterly* 28 (2014): 373–400.

———. *Martin Luthers Rhetorik des Herzens*. Tübingen: Mohr Siebeck, 2000.

Wengert, Timothy J. "The Biblical Commentaries of Philip Melanchthon." In *Philip Melanchthon (1497–1560) and the Commentary*, edited by Timothy J. Wengert and M. Patrick Graham, 106–48. Sheffield: Sheffield Academic Press, 1997.

———. "Building on the One Foundation with Straw: Martin Luther and the Epistle of James." *Word and World* 35 (2015): 251–61.

———. "Caspar Cruciger Sr.'s 1546 'Enarratio' on John's Gospel: An Experiment in Ecclesiological Exegesis." *Church History* 61 (1992): 60–74.

———. *Defending Faith: Lutheran Responses to Andreas Osiander's Doctrine of Justification*. Tübingen: Mohr Siebeck, 2012.

———. *A Formula for Parish Practice: Using the Formula of Concord in the Parish*. Grand Rapids: Eerdmans, 2006.

———. "Georg Major (1502–1574): Defender of the Wittenberg's Faith and Melanchthonian Exegete." In *Melanchthon in seinen Schülern*, edited by Heinz Scheible, 129–56. Wiesbaden: Harrassowitz, 1997.

———. *Human Freedom, Christian Righteousness: Philip Melanchthon's Exegetical Dispute with Erasmus of Rotterdam*. New York: Oxford University Press, 1998.

———. *Law and Gospel: Philip Melanchthon's Debate with John Agricola of Eisleben over "Poenitentia."* Grand Rapids: Baker, 1997.

———. *Martin Luther's Catechisms: Forming the Faith*. Minneapolis: Fortress Press, 2009.

———. "Martin Luther's *September Testament*: The Untold Story." *The Report: A Journal of German-American History* 47 (2017): 51–61.

———. "The 95 Theses as Luther's Template for Reading Scripture." *Lutheran Quarterly* 31 (2017): 249–66.

———. "A Note on 'Sola Scriptura' in Martin Luther's Writings." *Luther Bulletin* 20 (2011): 21–31.

———. "Philip Melanchthon and a Christian *Politics*." *Lutheran Quarterly* 17 (2003): 29–62.

———. "Philip Melanchthon and John Calvin against Andreas Osiander: Coming to Terms with Forensic Justification." In *Calvin and Luther: The Continuing Relationship*, edited by R. Ward Holder, 63–87. Göttingen: Vandenhoeck & Ruprecht, 2013.

———. *Philip Melanchthon's "Annotationes in Johannem" of 1523 in Relation to Its Predecessors and Contemporaries*. Geneva: Droz, 1987.

———. "Philip Melanchthon's 1522 Annotations on Romans and the Lutheran Origins of Rhetorical Criticism." In *Biblical Interpretation in the Era of the Reformation*, edited by Richard A. Muller and John L. Thompson, 118–40. Grand Rapids: Eerdmans, 1996.

———. *Reading the Bible with Martin Luther: An Introductory Guide*. Grand Rapids: Baker Academic, 2013.

Wengert, Timothy J., and M. Patrick Graham, eds. *Philip Melanchthon (1497–1560) and the Commentary*. Sheffield: Sheffield Academic, 1997.

Wengert, Timothy J., et al. "Report of a Working Group at the 1997 Luther Congress." *Luther-Jahrbuch* 66 (1999): 298–301.